JAMES STEWART

JAMES STEWART

A Pyramid Illustrated History of the Movies

by
HOWARD THOMPSON

General Editor: TED SENNETT

PUBLICATIONS
NEW YORK

For Bos of Princeton

JAMES STEWART
A Pyramid Illustrated History of the Movies

First edition published October, 1974

Photographs: Jerry Vermilye,
Movie Star News, and Cinemabilia

ISBN 0-515-03485-1

Library of Congress Catalog Card Number: 74-1590

Printed in the United States of America

Pyramid Books are published by Pyramid Communications, Inc. Its trademarks, consisting of the word "Pyramid" and the portrayal of a pyramid, are registered in the United States Patent Office.

Pyramid Communications, Inc., 919 Third Avenue, New York, N.Y. 10022

graphic design by anthony basile

ACKNOWLEDGMENTS

My editor on this project, Ted Sennett, proved to be an invaluable right-arm, and I should like to thank him accordingly.

CONTENTS

INTRODUCTION: JIMMY

Who is James Stewart? Simply, one of the best actors ever to come out of Hollywood, where he is still going strong as "Hawkins," a leading television sleuth snugly fitted into the Stewart persona. At sixty-six and 6 feet 3½ inches, James Maitland Stewart presents an impressive record as the son of a Pennsylvania hardware store owner, a Princeton graduate in architecture, an officer in the Air Force (he retired six years ago as a brigadier general in the Reserve), and a veteran of show business (ten plays and seventy-three films, including an Oscar). He is also a familiar figure on the Hollywood social scene where, married to one woman for twenty-five years, he quietly and steadily made movies that raked in millions while he became one of the film capital's richest citizens. Most people—moviegoers, film writers, friends and associates—think of him as Jimmy, not James. In the annals of the screen, where he is indelibly recorded as one of the best-known faces in the world, Stewart is unique.

He is one of the best actors alive. Watch "Hawkins" and study the Stewart eyes, a kind of window index to his entire career. True, the tailor-made attorney he portrays in this singularly adult television series carefully adheres to the familiar, homespun trademark that made Stewart famous: the hesitant, boyish gawkiness, the raspy drawl, the loose-jointed amble. Hawkins, we are reminded punctiliously as he solves those West Coast cases, is a native of West Virginia.

But those eyes, below a neat, discreetly gray toupee, burn intelligently like coals, heating up even more penetratingly when our hero closes in for the courtroom kill. This burrowing expression, exuding a fiercely honest, unswerving decency, denotes character, and it is the mature culmination of a professional actor at his peak. The Stewart image today is a man of character, of all-American flint and essential kindness. The metamorphosis of his career is laid out clearly night after night on television in his old films, from the naive, slow-talking youth who became the favorite son at glittery, star-laden Metro-Goldwyn-Mayer and went off to war with an Oscar for *The Philadelphia Story;* to the returned, honored, service veteran who played the film field independently, more selectively, more becomingly, in such character-developing roles as the dogged reporter of *Call Northside 777* (1948)

10

and the valiant baseball hero of *The Stratton Story* (1949); to the solidly comfortable star of Hitchcock thrillers and John Ford Westerns; to the aging but still rugged and justice-minded figure in sixties Westerns. Gently and laconically, his comedy style, charmingly evidenced in prewar films like *The Shop Around the Corner* (1940) and *Come Live With Me* (1941), had also taken on a subtler edge over the years, as in *Harvey* (1950) and even *Bell, Book and Candle* (1958). And in a film such as *Anatomy of a Murder* (1959), he brilliantly blended *all* facets of his acting skill in a portrayal of a buzz-saw lawyer that won him a citation from the New York Film Critics. This role was a forerunner of the "Hawkins" to come.

And with *Hawkins* now piping him anew into millions of American homes as a household word, Stewart is one of the few major Hollywood stars to have latched onto a television series that has won both public and critical acclaim. Julie Andrews, for instance, in her tasteful musical series that won critical plaudits, flopped disastrously in the audience ratings. But Fred MacMurray, on the other hand, did well in a comedy series that nobody seemed to take seriously but millions watched. Barbara Stanwyck also did well with her Western image in *The Big Valley*. Topping them all in popularity, ironically, was *Marcus Welby's* Robert Young, who was not in the major star category before television. For that matter such people as Buddy Ebsen, Carroll O'Connor, Gene Barry, Hugh O'Brian and James Arness were minor Hollywood figures, hanging on the ropes for years, before television skyrocketed them to fame.

Stewart already had the fame, not to say fortune. He has worked at it long and hard.

Curiously, James Stewart's movie career has flourished over a remarkable span of years, with a reasonable number of failures, for an actor devoid of one iota of what is known as sex appeal. Hollywood demanded it, in some form or another, back in the thirties when Stewart arrived. With his thin frame and boyish appeal, Stewart had none of the personal aura that is supposed to make hearts flutter, although his prewar career found him paired with such estimable belles as Ginger Rogers, Lana Turner, Carole Lombard, Katharine Hepburn and Hedy Lamarr.

Acting aside, male glamour was a prime requisite for a leading man at MGM, Stewart's early home base, from Clark Gable to Van Johnson. At other studios, John Wayne, Cary Grant, Gary Cooper, Henry Fonda, Spencer Tracy, Errol Flynn, James Cagney and later stars like Gregory Peck and Burt Lancaster, all managed to project a brand of virility considered commensurate with talent. Not skinny Jimmy.

An aura of youthful innocence and decency may have been the next best thing to sex appeal. These two qualities are obvious in an early photograph of Stewart, squeezing an accordion, singing and flanked by classmates during a musical show put on by the Princeton Triangle Club students in 1930. Stewart has described his boyhood years as "av-

THE EARLY YEARS: THE MURDER MAN TO MR. SMITH

erage." Born on May 20, 1908 in Indiana, Pennsylvania, a small town where his father ran a hardware store, young Stewart attended Mercersburg Academy, then Princeton University, where he became interested in theater but majored in architecture, winning a bachelor of science degree.

"I was interested in architecture," Stewart recalls. "But I guess I wasn't interested enough." After graduation, he joined a schoolmate, Joshua Logan (later the famed director), at Falmouth, Massachusetts, where Logan formed the University Players troupe which included Henry Fonda (later Stewart's roommate in Manhattan and in Hollywood) and Margaret Sullavan (a future co-star in three movies). Within the next few years, Stewart appeared on Broadway, playing small roles in *Carrie Nation*, *All Good Americans* and *Yellow Jack*. Hedda Hopper, touring with Stewart in a summer theater version of *Divided by Three*, is supposed to have signaled MGM about the young actor's capabilities, resulting in a seven-year contract with the studio, beginning in 1935.

Stewart's first film was *The Murder Man*, a flimsy, contrived

14

Jimmy at age four

Young Jimmy

ROSE MARIE (1936). With Jeanette MacDonald

mystery-melodrama, with Spencer Tracy as an intrepid reporter who solves a crime. Young Jimmy, billed in sixth place, played Shorty, a colleague of Tracy's. He was next seen briefly hiding in a Canadian mountain cabin, as the outlaw brother of Jeanette MacDonald in *Rose Marie* (1936), the studio's second operetta teaming the soprano with Nelson Eddy. Stewart's role was small, but a key one in the plot, and at least he was seen distinctly in a popular success, as "Mountie" Eddy closed in with handcuffs. And the studio proceeded to keep Stewart hopping with five more assignments during 1936.

Reportedly at the request of Margaret Sullavan, who had just made a luminous screen debut in Universal's *Only Yesterday*, he was loaned out as her co-star in *Next Time We Love*. Directed by Edward H. Griffith, this was a fairly vapid romantic drama concerning the rocky marriage of a Broadway star (Sullavan) and a roving journalist (Stewart). The faithful friend of the couple, billed third, was Ray Milland.

Stewart's fourth film was another top-notch production back at Metro, the surprisingly smooth and entertaining *Wife vs. Secretary*, with Myrna Loy and Jean Harlow politely tugging over Clark Gable amid glistening Cedric Gibbons sets. In such swank company, billed sixth, young Stewart held his own adequately as the faithful, standby suitor of Miss Harlow. (The actress' platinum-blonde tresses were dyed a subdued brown to match her rather subdued and attractive performance as Gable's devoted secretary.) Then came another sixth billing for Stewart in *Small Town Girl*, innocuously pleasant fluff out of a Ben Ames Williams novel, with Janet Gaynor inspiring Robert Taylor to change his playboy ways; Stewart appeared as a local yokel named Elmer. Then he starred, for the first time, in a minor film, *Speed*, playing a test driver in an automobile plant, with Wendy Barrie as the boss' daughter and the Indianapolis Speedway for a racing climax. Quickie or no quickie, Stewart had drawn his initial top billing, over Miss Barrie.

There now materialized an overdressed and overstuffed disaster titled *The Gorgeous Hussy*, a Joan Crawford fantasy tenuously moored to the presidential career of Andrew Jackson, in which Stewart, though billed sixth, was literally lost among a good, milling cast, including Lionel Barrymore, Franchot Tone, Melvyn Douglas and Beulah Bondi. Miss Crawford's co-star was the studio's new glamour boy, Robert Taylor, a shining contrast to the thin, Ichabod Crane-like Stewart, portraying a minor, rustic character named "Rowdy" Dow. But at least Stewart had been seen in a prestige failure.

He had also caught the eye of no less than Cole Porter, who suggested him as leading man opposite Eleanor Powell, a smiling, staccato

NEXT TIME WE LOVE (1936). With Margaret Sullavan and Ray Milland

WIFE VS. SECRETARY (1936). With Jean Harlow

tapper, in *Born To Dance*, a cheerful, gleaming extravaganza with lilting Porter music, the composer's first original score for the screen. In this enjoyable musical, Stewart's eighth role (his seventh in 1936), his career was finally on firm ground as hero of a good, major film. As a Navy gob, he played easily and naturally. He even sang, pleasantly enough, in several ensemble numbers and introduced "Easy To Love," one of the film's two best tunes. (The other was "I've Got You Under My Skin" sung by Virginia Bruce, as a volatile Broadway actress.) It was an entertaining show blithely directed by Roy Del Ruth,

and a propitious showcase for the rising Stewart.

It did young Jimmy no harm at all, in fact, to have been centered so prominently as leading man in a popular sunburst of an MGM musical like *Born to Dance*. He had Porter personally to thank for his casting, judging by the composer's diary excerpts. Most of the project had already been cast when Porter suggested Stewart. The studio "thought the idea was most interesting, if Stewart could sing." The next day the young actor came to Porter's house to audition and the composer wrote: "He sings far from well, although he has nice notes in his

THE GORGEOUS HUSSY (1936). With Joan Crawford

voice, but he could play the part perfectly."*

Stewart certainly played it well enough, adding an occasional look of edgy, awed shyness not usually associated with the hero of a big musical. And the project rolled ahead before the cameras, with the studio confident of another Navy-based hit, especially after the success of RKO's *Follow the Fleet*, with Ginger Rogers and Fred Astaire. (This time the gobs are on shore leave from a submarine.) Early in the film, Stewart stepped comfortably into line with the others—Miss Powell, Frances Langford, Buddy Ebsen, Una Merkel and Sid Silvers—for "Hey, Babe, Hey!" a honky-tonk-waltz

*George Eells, *The Life That Late He Led*, G. Putnam's Sons, New York, 1967, p. 161.

clog. When Stewart's big musical moment came, with the haunting "Easy to Love," he perched on a park bench and chanted both verse and chorus to Miss Powell in a sweetly husky voice, before the dancer, with her perennial, open-mouthed smile and electric footwork, went into a rhapsodic spin. (This was followed by a burlesque pantomime-conducting of the number by Reginald Gardiner, as a strolling park policeman.)

Nobody who ever saw *Born to Dance* could ever forget the eye-popping finale, "Swinging the Jinx Away," a glittering number set aboard a stage-revue battleship with all the trimmings. Miss Langford sings the rhythmic song, then the camera soars to the highest turret for a caped and spangled Miss

Powell, who then spirals down winding steps and takes over the ship with those clattering tap shoes. As the number ends, the dancer flips into a standing salute, flanked by the ship's ensemble, and the ship's long-range guns boom smoke straight into the camera.*

As the studio's juiciest musical plum of the year, *Born to Dance* hurt no one in it, least of all James Stewart. However, MGM now wedged him into *After the Thin Man*, an adequate follow-up to the successful, first *Thin Man* film, dominated by those popular charmers, William Powell and Myrna Loy. The surprise here was Stewart's unmasking as the killer, in a climax that had his boyish features rather intriguingly twisted, for a change, into a snarl. This was a small, neat vignette that becomingly sandpapered some of the rising young actor's all-American halo, indicating versatility. This was Stewart's eighth movie in that one year, 1936.

The wheel turned: two failures. The larger one was *Seventh Heaven* (1937), a tepid 20th Century-Fox

*The best *forgotten* tune in Porter's fine score is his sparkling, adroit "Love Me, Love My Pekingese," which Virginia Bruce sings to thread her publicity reception aboard the ship.

BORN TO DANCE (1936). With Sid Silvers and Una Merkel

remake of the silent classic that had starred Janet Gaynor and Charles Farrell, now with that studio's baby-faced import, Simone Simon, as a pouting, mannered Paris waif and Stewart (on loan-out) as her beloved chimneysweep. Everything went wrong here, including the actor's "remarkably adenoidal voice," as one reviewer put it. Gale Sondergaard stole the show, a case of petty larceny, as the heroine's nasty sister. Little could be said of MGM's *The Last Gangster* (1937), a hard-breathing melodrama dominated by a growling Edward G. Robinson, although a Viennese import named Rose Stradner and Stewart, as a sympathetic journalist, performed with subdued ease.

Now came two worthy, medium-sized human-interest dramas. *Navy Blue and Gold* (1937) had all

BORN TO DANCE (1936). With Eleanor Powell

AFTER THE THIN MAN (1936). With William Powell and Sam Levene

SEVENTH HEAVEN (1937).
With Simone Simon

the earmarks of another "rah-rah" service story about Annapolis brass-buttoned middies. But the picture was warm, it moved crisply and the tone and playing were agreeable, with Stewart, Robert Young and Tom Brown as roommates whose adventures and misadventures led inevitably to a climactic football game. Under Sam Wood's relaxed direction, Stewart gave an ingratiating performance as the most likable of the trio. Florence Rice and Lionel Barrymore (as the indispensable old seadog) provided sturdy support.

Of Human Hearts (1938) cut deeper, often brilliantly, as the story of an American frontier family, under the sagacious direction of Clarence Brown. The film featured a cluster of superb performances, with Walter Huston and Beulah Bondi as pioneer parents and Stewart and young Gene Reynolds as farm boys.

Few previous films, in fact, had dramatized a backwoods clan with such moving dignity and conviction. There were a few melodramatic spurts but generally the fine screen play by Bradbury Foote bypassed the traditional clichés accorded screen frontiersmen and held to the simple, human values of one wilderness family. Huston was splendid as the stern, religious father, at odds with the rebellious, confused boy portrayed by Stewart.

And Miss Bondi was superb as the mother who tirelessly sacrificed to send the thoughtless Stewart through medical school.

In one of the best scenes, near the end, Stewart is summoned from the front line by no less than President Lincoln (John Carradine), scolded and sent home. There were also fine sideline performances by Guy Kibbee as a storekeeper and Charles Coburn as a village doctor.

Now that Stewart had scored so impressively in a budding, Lincolnesque category, he was given a good contrast in his next assignment, *Vivacious Lady* (1938). This RKO comedy, teaming Ginger Rogers and Stewart, was fine, bubbly fun in a college setting, with Stewart as a shy associate professor of botany who brings home an irrepressible bride from New York. The zestful girl, whom Stewart first meets in a night club, proceeds to tilt the campus and also thwarts her husband's scheming ex-girlfriend, played by Frances Mercer. Stewart and the vivacious Ginger were perfectly cast, as were Charles Coburn and Beulah Bondi, who gave them keen, mature competition as Stewart's parents. The movie coasted along delightfully under George Stevens' skilled direction. Two things were close to memorable—one was a campus party scene, with a close-up of Miss Bondi's swinging derriere, as

NAVY BLUE AND GOLD (1937). With Robert Young and Tom Brown

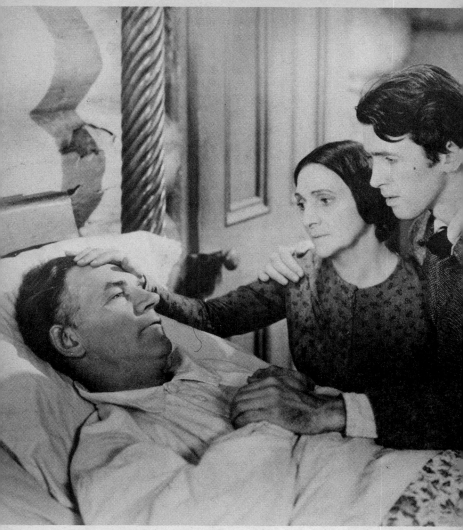

OF HUMAN HEARTS (1938). With Walter Huston and Beulah Bondi

VIVACIOUS LADY (1938). With Ginger Rogers

she gamely undertook the dance rage of the moment, the Big Apple. The other pearl was Ginger's wisecrack, as she and Miss Bondi watch the scheming Miss Mercer clutch Stewart on the dance floor. "Kinda close to him, isn't she?" murmurs Miss Bondi. Says Ginger, grimly: "If she gets any closer to him, she'll be behind him."

This successful lark was followed by a rather dreary, contrived remake, back at MGM, of *The Shopworn Angel* (1938). The original Paramount movie had Nancy Carroll and Gary Cooper and a tune that became a popular song of the day and summarized the theme of the drama perfectly: "The Precious Little Thing Called Love." In the new version, Margaret Sullavan was the showgirl mystically smitten with a fairly dim-witted Army private about to be shipped overseas during World War I. Neither Stewart nor his co-star could surmount this tearful business. Standing by merely to express sympathy, Walter Pidgeon had it easier. H.C. Potter provided the sluggish direction.

Better luck came for Stewart in a choice casting in a major comedy at Columbia, where director Frank Capra and scenarist Robert Riskin were assembling an adaptation of *You Can't Take It With You* (1938), the Pulitzer Prize-winning stage comedy by George S. Kaufman and Moss Hart. Stewart proved to be effective as a rich man's son in love with the daughter of a lovably eccentric family. The cast was carefully hand-picked. The film intelligently expanded and fleshed out the simpler and slightly broader stage blueprint; Capra and his cast did the rest, starting with Lionel Barrymore as the plain-talking patriarch of the Sycamore clan, and Jean Arthur as his unspoiled granddaughter.

As the plot amusingly underscored the penniless bliss of the zany Sycamore household, the film exuded an all-American glow of comfort and security derived from simple, solid human values—the Capra trademark. Under the director's aegis, Stewart was to become the personal quintessence of such values and ideals, front and center, in two of his best vehicles, *Mr. Smith Goes to Washington* and *It's a Wonderful Life* (which both Stewart and Capra have called their own favorite movie).

Seen today, *You Can't Take It With You* bulges more than a bit, as though Capra and Riskin had tried to cram in too much of everything, from common sense to sunshine. A Broadway revival of the play in 1965, minus the Hollywood trimmings, forcefully suggested the charming eccentricity and uncluttered structure of the Kaufman and Hart original.

THE SHOPWORN ANGEL (1938)
With Margaret Sullavan

YOU CAN'T TAKE IT WITH YOU (1938). With Jean Arthur, Samuel S. Hinds, Halliwell Hobbes, and Donald Meek. At left: Mary Forbes

While young Stewart and Miss Arthur could hardly have been more appealing as the young sweethearts, some of their scenes now seem pasted into the middle of the film with a determined thumb. At one point, the young couple quietly steal away from the milling confusion in the Sycamore home and sit on a park bench. They look at each other adoringly, then Stewart begins a speech on the importance of simple values. "Now here," he drawls, "is a blade of grass." He holds one up, with pinched fingers. This entire scene, including young Jimmy, now seems more than a bit arch and sticky.

So does the film's ending, with the entire cast spilling out of the Sycamore home into the street singing "For He's a Jolly Good Fellow," as the entire neighborhood joins in to pay homage to Grandpa who has saved them all from being uprooted.

Nevertheless, Hollywood's version of *You Can't Take It With You* was immensely entertaining. In addition to Barrymore, Stewart, Miss Arthur and Edward Arnold, as Stewart's rich but unhappy father, there were Spring Byington as the darling but dense mother (originated on the stage by Josephine Hull), Ann Miller as her second daughter, a ballet-skirted twirler, Mischa Auer as her caustic teacher

YOU CAN'T TAKE IT WITH YOU (1938). With Ann Miller, Jean Arthur, and Mischa Auer

MADE FOR EACH OTHER (1939).
With Carole Lombard

("Confidentially, she stinks"), Donald Meek, Samuel S. Hinds, Halliwell Hobbes, Mary Forbes and Eddie "Rochester" Anderson, all adding to the original spirit of the play, which remained at the center of the film.

Mr. Smith Goes to Washington, the next, even more successful collaboration of Capra, Stewart and Miss Arthur, came after three Stewart vehicles ranging from top-notch to the dregs.

Two young people get married, have a child, experience mother-in-law trouble, servant problems, then finally a critical illness that is climaxed by a plane's winging through a storm to deliver a life-saving serum to their baby. This was the plot of *Made For Each Other* (1939), co-starring Stewart and Carole Lombard. The movie also happened to have an exceptionally tasteful production by the independent David O. Selznick, an unforced and observant screenplay by Jo Swerling, excellent direction by John Cromwell and beautifully understanding performances by the entire cast. Of the supporting players, Lucile Watson was espe-

ICE FOLLIES OF 1939 (1939). With Joan Crawford

IT'S A WONDERFUL WORLD (1939). With Claudette Colbert

cially fine as the pushy mother-in-law. Though teetering on the edge of banality, the film's tone and treatment rendered the familiar not only credible but highly appealing.

The last sequence of this United Artists release, with Miss Lombard and Stewart enduring the crucial wait for the arrival of the plane that would save their child, was given astonishing authenticity by two players who had not experienced parenthood themselves.

Ice Follies of 1939, vaguely fired off in the direction of the box office and 20th Century-Fox, where Sonja Henie was a popular favorite, was a gaudy and indigestible pastiche of cornmeal and bubble gum, with some fair sideline skating and another rocky-marriage plot involving Joan Crawford, posing on skates with her hair dyed jet black, and Stewart, who with Lew Ayres was called upon to frolic in a horse's costume. Even the color photography of the film's extravagant finale was poor.

The odd fact about *It's a Wonderful World* (1939), pairing Stewart and Claudette Colbert (in a rare stint on the MGM lot), is that few people seem to recall it. The reviews were less than enthusiastic for this whirl-away comedy, which arrived rather belatedly at the end of a cycle of screwball romps. Yet the film's occasional surfacing on television re-

MR. SMITH GOES TO WASHINGTON (1939). With Jean Arthur

eals it to be a clever and funny arce with definite virtues, starting with the picaresque brine and bite of Ben Hecht's script, as Miss Colbert, playing a pert poetess, and Stewart, a gangling scoutmaster, ripped around the countryside, involved with two murders, a private eye, two homicide-bureau comics and even a barn theater company. The film also moves as briskly as a country rabbit, under the direction of W. S. Van Dyke.

For *Mr. Smith Goes to Washington* (1939), Stewart moved back to director Frank Capra at Columbia. It is one of the actor's best-known roles and certainly one of his outstanding performances, winning him his first award by the New York Film Critics, although not the coveted Oscar of the Academy of Motion Picture Arts and Sciences which went that year to Robert Donat for *Goodbye, Mr. Chips*).

Here was another ambitious, full-rigged comedy from Capra, packed with satirical bite but loaded in favor of courage, sentiment and justice, as a naive, idealistic young senator valiantly takes on a pack of crooked political leaders in the nation's capital. Beautifully paced and balanced by Capra, with a fine screenplay by Sidney Buchman, the picture is essentially a plea for honesty and decency, even while cocking an amusing, sardonic eye at the Washington arena (where the film was received less than appreciatively).

Stewart was splendid in the starring role, with solid support from Jean Arthur, Claude Rains, Edward Arnold, Thomas Mitchell and others in the teeming cast. The picture was immensely successful. Watching it more than three decades later, it is impossible to imagine any one other than Stewart as Mr. Smith (a blood brother to Capra's earlier *Mr. Deeds*, played by Gary Cooper). In these times of government scandal and exposure, the movie has real thrust in asserting, the American way, that right will inevitably rout might.

The film holds up now as a beautifully crafted endeavor, blending warmth, sentiment, comedy and laced with political savvy and cynicism. (Way back when, the cynicism seemed more scathing.) It is also superbly written, played and piloted; the idealist-hero who now emerges triumphant over corruption, as personified and played to the hilt by young Stewart in his most memorable, prewar tour de force, seems even more admirable today. His behavior now appears more realistic and less that of a do-gooder goaded into action.

After *Mr. Deeds Goes to Town*, Capra had again wanted to use Gary Cooper, who had other commitments, for his young political protagonist in *Mr. Smith*, which Buch-

MR. SMITH GOES TO WASHINGTON (1939). Jeff Smith's filibuster

man shaped into a screenplay (an Oscar-winner) from Lewis R. Foster's story, "The Man From Montana." But Stewart, with his own unsullied, homespun image, was perfect, from the early part of the movie, when he arrives in Washington to fill a senatorial appointment and gawks at the historical landmarks and buildings, to the fadeout, when his dogged, one-man filibuster draws a thunderous ovation in the Senate.

The story moves crisply, as Edward Arnold, the powerful political boss, and Claude Rains, the corrupt senator from the newcomer's home state (unspecified, other than western), try to hoodwink Stewart over a graft deal, then malign the hard-headed young idealist. There are many outstanding scenes, such as the gullible newcomer's mischievous roasting by the Washington press; in a touchingly imaginative scene that just escapes banality, Stewart visits the Lincoln Memorial in his time of deepest despair, forsaken by his colleagues. Capra drew exceptionally forceful performances from his entire cast. Miss Arthur was superb as Stewart's wise, tart-tongued secretary who first sees him as a well-meaning boob and comes to love him. She is even more appealing and credible here than with her somewhat similar characterization in *Mr. Deeds*. There is a piercing moment of drama when she shouts encouragement over the gallery railing as Stewart exhaustedly lags in his de-

MR. SMITH GOES TO WASHINGTON (1939). With Claude Rains

termined, marathon filibuster.

But the great drama—and heartbeat—of *Mr. Smith Goes to Washington* is the filibuster itself, with the haggard, hoarse-voiced Stewart persevering for attention from the initially bored, sparsely filled assembly, as the camera pulls in close to magnify his desperation and pulls back to dwarf the lone, fighting man in bleak perspective. Cut into this footage, like splintery, sunbeam assurances that right will somehow prevail, are marvelously effective close-ups of Harry Carey, whose kind, smiling countenance at the presiding bench of the Senate provides the stubborn youth's only nearby encouragement.

Right does make might, of course, at least here, and it is almost a relief when Stewart finally croaks, "I'm going to stay right here and fight for this lost cause," then keels over in a faint. It is an emotion-charged climax to a memorable film.

Capra, perhaps a bit naively, proudly arranged and attended the film's premiere in Washington, a dressy occasion crowded with prominent politicians and the press corps, most of whom were aghast at the less-than-rose-colored depiction of the nation's capital behind the scenes.

Elsewhere the reviews and box-office response were highly favorable. The testy, independent New York Film Critics, who couldn't have cared less about their miffed counterparts in Washington, named Stewart the best actor of 1939.

As one of Hollywood's foremost young performers, with a bright all-American feather in his cap for *Mr. Smith Goes to Washington*, Stewart now made his first Western, *Destry Rides Again* (1939), opening up a new segment of his career. It was an enormous hit, and a delightful film. It was also an ideal follow-up, giving him a "Smith"-like role, as a moralistic, anti-violence deputy pitted against the corruption of a prairie town centered in the Bloody Gulch saloon. Stewart's natural portrayal meshed easily with that of his co-star, Marlene Dietrich, as the lusty saloon singer, in an earthy appearance that did the actress worlds of good.

Weighed under for years by the artistic gauze and paraphernalia of rather remote sophistication, Miss Dietrich had found herself abruptly called Hollywood box-office poison at a theater exhibitors' convention. (So, for that matter, was Katharine Hepburn, whose salvation was *The Philadelphia Story*.)

Everything clicked in *Destry*, surprisingly so since most of the ingredients were as dusty as the background, a wild frontier hamlet named Bottleneck. But the Felix Jackson-Gertrude Purcell-Henry Myers adaptation of Max Brand's novel was a viable one for the likes of Stewart, Miss Dietrich and the experienced director, George Marshall, who moved the story at a neat,

BEYOND MR. SMITH: FROM DESTRY TO THE WAR YEARS

tangy clip. The players, equipped with some tart, tongue-in-cheek lingo for a streamlined old West, made the most of their roles. Stewart, of course, was just right for the mild-mannered but fearless new sheriff. But this Universal project was really Miss Dietrich's, as she attempted a comeback on an unaccustomed Western trail and proceeded to shine like a tawdry diamond in the role of the feathered saloon sharpie, whether singing "See What the Boys In the Back Room Will Have" or "Little Joe" or pitching into one of the roughest female fights ever filmed, with Una Merkel as her sparring partner.

Stewart now returned to MGM for *The Shop Around the Corner* (1940), with director Ernst Lubitsch piloting a light, delectable story about the salespeople and owner of a medium-sized store in Budapest. The most curious aspect of this film, with its distinctly Continental milieu, was the grace and credibility of the playing by such un-Continental types as Stewart and Margaret Sullavan (as two clerks unwittingly engaged in a pen-pal correspondence), blustery Frank Morgan (the proprietor),

DESTRY RIDES AGAIN (1939). With Marlene Dietrich

Sara Haden, William Tracy, and the others. Joseph Schildkraut, the wily villain on the premises, *did* seem Hungarian. Much of Samson Raphaelson's delightful screenplay (adapted from a play by Nikolaus Laszlo) takes place in Matuscheck & Company, the kind of store that doesn't exist any more (or may never have existed), with its deferential salespeople and vaguely paternal proprietor.

Before Lubitsch closes in on the heart of the plot, handled with his usual delicacy and charm, the director has evoked his background with nicely detailed intimacy and dignity, such as the ritual of each day's shop-opening. The fly in this cozy setup is Proprietor Morgan's gradual suspicion that Clerk Stewart is having an affair with his wife (unseen); it's really Schildkraut. Stewart, a gentle, noble chap, is only having an anonymous letter-exchange with his dream girl, who, unknown to both, works at his side. This, of course, is Miss Sullavan.

The two stars are utterly disarming and so is the tender tone sustained by their director as the pen-pal "romance" progresses. There is, for instance, the scene of their first scheduled meeting in a restaurant, involving a carnation and a copy of *Anna Karenina*, or the lovely, touching bit when we simply see Miss Sullavan's hand forlornly exploring a letter rack for a crucial missive that hasn't arrived. Everything here worked easily and becomingly, even with Stewart looking and sounding more like a native of Indiana, Pennsylvania, than a citizen of Budapest, Hungary. But Budapest never had a more appealing shop, at least in a Hollywood movie.

Time has outweighed the critical verdict of *The New York Times* on *The Mortal Storm* (1940) as essentially "blistering anti-Nazi propaganda" that was "grim and depressing." It was also considerably more and still is. Set in Munich, in a small university community, the film, based on Phyllis Bottome's novel, showed how early Nazism shattered and divided a loving fam-

ily and finally routed two freethinking young people (Stewart and Miss Sullavan again). The film ends in death, with the boy cradling the girl in his arms on a border ski slope after a rain of Nazi bullets.

Compared to later events, the Nazi holocaust that tilted the world, the film now seems not only perceptively intelligent but even restrained in its unleashing of brutality and venom. Nor do the other characters seem exaggerated on the sides of good and evil, as played by Robert Young, Frank Morgan, Robert Stack, Irene Rich, Bonita

DESTRY RIDES AGAIN (1939). With Marlene Dietrich

THE SHOP AROUND THE CORNER (1940). With Margaret Sullavan and Frank Morgan

THE SHOP AROUND THE CORNER (1940). With Margaret Sullavan

Granville, Maria Ouspenskaya and Gene Reynolds. This fine cast responded well to the searching direction of Frank Borzage and the imaginative screenplay by Claudine West, Andersen Ellis, and George Froeschel.

The opening, for instance, and its later match-up, is brilliantly handled as we see Morgan, a deeply respected professor, briskly striding alone through the university halls to his classroom. He opens the door and stands stunned by an eruption of applause, a birthday tribute, from a room crammed with students, faculty and his family. There is a repeat of the fade-in about two-thirds into the drama, after the aging teacher has been officially ostracized because of "non-Aryan blood" and two stepsons (Young and Stack) have become ardent Nazi followers. Now we see Morgan striding through the same halls, shunned, and opening the door on a virtually empty classroom.

Borzage and the writer also inject an exquisite bit of pantomime that signifies the satanic rumble of the onrushing "mortal storm." This is a scene in a tavern in which a drinking song suddenly turns into a saluting, heil-Hitler rendition of the German national anthem. As the crowd feverishly

THE MORTAL STORM (1940). With Bonita Granville, Margaret Sullavan, and Maria Ouspenskaya

THE MORTAL STORM (1940). With Dan Dailey, Jr. (soldier facing him)

peals out the tribute to Nazism, the camera quietly seeks out a small, gentle-looking old man simply standing in the rear, hat in hand and head bowed. Now he is spotted by the uniformed Nazis, most of them youths; they viciously pummel him to the floor.

The story moves forward grippingly, with the home of the Roth family left empty and desolate; with the father sent to a concentration camp; with the courageous daughter, Miss Sullavan, and her idealistic sweetheart, Stewart, forced to flee over the mountains on skis, only to find death in the snow. Somehow, this graphically poignant ending conveyed a note of hope and a tribute to the universal human spirit, crushed but not destroyed by the terrible reality. The film stands as a strong, touching Hollywood preview of one of the blackest chapters in history.

Next, in *No Time For Comedy* (1940), Stewart faced a less than world-shaking question: Does a successful Broadway actress, Rosalind Russell, keep her playwright husband, Stewart, from turning serious and social-minded under the influence of a comely rival? The Julius J. and Philip G. Epstein script, based on S.N. Behrman's stage hit with Katharine Cornell and Laurence Olivier (not exactly a Stewart type), opened up the story more romantically and

humorously, rendering Behrman's intellectual caper far cozier than it had been onstage.

The movie was much more spontaneous and earthy, especially in the new, early scenes as the clumsily ingratiating playwright is first exposed to Broadway and his new star. Stewart stole the show but Miss Russell's typically bright, collected cool was a perfect counterpart.

Under William Keighley's lighthearted direction, the development of the story made bouncily amusing entertainment. The original play was a brightly arch, slightly strained bauble with one elegant drawing-room set unsurprisingly dominated by the majestic Miss Cornell; young Olivier was slimly, handsomely British and properly naive as he bobbed in her wake. The Behrman dialogue was linked like precise, polished pearls. But the movie, with its change of equal time for both stars, was funny where the play was amusing. And the performances by the stars and by Charles Ruggles as the bemused husband of Stewart's "patroness" (Genevieve Tobin), helped to make the film more spontaneously attractive than the caviar-flavored original.

Following this stint at Warners, Stewart returned to MGM to appear in one of his most successful films. *The Philadelphia Story* (1940) was a merrily fizzing cocktail that

NO TIME FOR COMEDY (1940). As Gaylord Esterbrook

benefited every one concerned and officially put Hollywood's top seal of approval, the Oscar, on Stewart as crown prince of Hollywood's most prestigious studio.

Gable was still king. Stewart was not to be confused with the more glamorous Robert Taylor. Nor had any of the studio's promotion even hinted at sex appeal; for that matter, how could it? With the simplest and wisest logic, MGM had decided to fully back an Oscar nomination for unadulterated acting by its most favored young character actor. Jimmy didn't even get the girl in this film, but he won the prize that really mattered.

It was a triumph for Stewart, and yet the film has become virtually synonymous with Miss Hepburn. The plain truth, however, is that the great Kate had sidled back to Hollywood. It was a triumphant sidling, true. Her RKO career had floundered, whereupon she returned East to conquer Broadway (as never before) with a long, successful run and tour of this upper-crust charade written for her by Philip Barry. Obviously determined to prolong her success, Miss Hepburn bought the movie rights herself and presented the package to MGM, which eagerly snapped it up, with her in the starring role. (Does any one remember that Stewart's role of the sharp-tongued reporter was originated on Broadway by Van Heflin? Or that the Cary Grant role of the ex-husband who reclaims his wife was originally Joseph Cotten's?)

In a cold light, the plot of *The Philadelphia Story* is gossamer fluff.

THE PHILADELPHIA STORY (1940). With Ruth Hussey, Katharine Hepburn, and Mary Nash

THE PHILADELPHIA STORY (1940).
With Katharine Hepburn

It's brilliant, granted—the performing of all, the literate script by Donald Ogden Stewart, the chocolate-smooth direction by George Cukor—but *The Philadelphia Story* has feet of clay. For all its charm and dazzlingly sophisticated savvy and appointments, this movie—and the play—is about the melting of a priggish, rather obnoxious young society divorcée.

But who would be dull and grim enough to x-ray a cocktail if it tastes delicious? *The Philadelphia Story* did. It slides past lusciously now on television, when uncut; all those marvelous scenes and gleaming snippets of dialogue intact, as, for instance, Grant's husky-voiced, fond reminiscences of their early nuptial bliss to a seemingly indignant Miss Hepburn. He remembers their honeymoon boat, the *True Love*, and suddenly the lady weakens: "My, she was so *yar*."

Rather oddly, in her television conversation with Dick Cavett, Miss Hepburn said she didn't remember the details of the movie's opening, which was pure, delightful pantomime indicating the previous breakup of the Grant-Hepburn marriage. At the front door, Miss Hepburn furiously smashes Grant's golf club. Without a wasted motion, Grant stalks up to her and virtually slams her out of sight. Cavett asked Miss Hepburn how the fall was

THE PHILADELPHIA STORY (1940). With John Howard, Cary Grant and Katharine Hepburn

cushioned. Untypically, she shrugged vaguely.

Effective as this introductory pantomime was, it supplanted one of this writer's favorite first lines of a Broadway play, which opens with the heroine, Tracy Lord, her mother and little sister immersed in the paperwork preparations for Tracy's second wedding. (John Howard played this forgotten man on the screen.) Tracy looks up and asks: "How many m's in omelet?"

The Barry play had taken place in a drawing room and on a poolside terrace, but naturally Hollywood wasn't about to have its film cast so confined. Hence the film moves about that creamy tasteful MGM house, complete with swimming pool, which the studio not only used for scores of subsequent movies—it was immediately recognizable—but had ready for use again in 1956 when *The Philadelphia Story* became the musical, *High Society.*

The excellent Donald Ogden Stewart script expanded the action across the grounds and even, in a charmingly imaginative touch, to the local library for a scene in which

COME LIVE WITH ME (1941). With Hedy Lamarr

POT O' GOLD (1941). With Paulette Goddard

the other Stewart, Jimmy, finds Miss Hepburn reading some of his articles. "I've looked you up," she tells him, smiling and obviously impressed. Later, in a well-remembered night scene at poolside, as Stewart exclaims that she is a "golden girl, full of life and warmth and delight," she is clearly more than impressed.

In March 1941, Stewart ambled forward, clad in a tuxedo, to receive his award from the Academy of Motion Picture Arts and Sciences for the best male starring performance of the previous year. Alongside him was Ginger Rogers, cited for *Kitty Foyle*. The presenters were no less than Alfred Lunt and Lynn Fontanne. Newsreel clips of the Academy banquet at the Los Angeles Biltmore are interesting to see now. Stewart, looking his shy, sincere self, made a brief, becoming acceptance speech; Lunt was paternal and benign. A tearful Ginger, calling it "the happiest moment of my life," received a queenly kiss on the forehead from Miss Fontanne.

What lay ahead for James Stewart after achieving this top acting honor? Nothing formidable, as it happened. He more or less marked time placidly in three films before going off to war. It's just possible that the studio didn't quite know what to do with him. Hence they cast him in *Come Live With Me* (1941), a light comedy opposite Hedy Lamarr, with Stewart as a footloose writer and the alluring Hedy as a refugee who avoids deportation by marrying him. Love, of course, finds a way.

Come Live With Me is one of those bygone baubles that seems effortless and more entertaining on television than it did originally. The two stars do quite nicely by the material, a screenplay which Patterson McNutt based on a story by Virginia Van Upp. The opening scene, for instance, has an immediate, appealing ring of conviction, as Stewart protests that a dime he has placed on the counter of an all-night diner has been filched; Miss Lamarr, seated next to him, speaks up in his defense. Ejected, the two strangers leave the diner together. Clarence Brown's direction was persuasively relaxed and so was the smooth playing of Ian Hunter, as the married publisher Hedy professes to love, Verree Teasdale as his wife, Donald Meek, and Barton MacLane.

Whatever possessed Stewart to appear in (or MGM to lend him for) *Pot o' Gold* (1941), a United Artists release co-starring Paulette Goddard, is a mystery. A frank cash-in on the popular radio program featuring Horace Heidt and his orchestra, the film was a jumble of tired gags and even more tired song-and-dance and standard interludes by the Heidt band. Stewart,

ZIEGFELD GIRL (1941). With Lana Turner

Brigadier General Stewart, wearing the flight line cap of his old squadron in World War II.

with his twisted smile, gave punch to a few lines. Miss Goddard, Charles Winninger and the others fared worse.

Unscathed, at least, Stewart now slipped quietly, perfectly respectably, into a sideline role as the faithful, humble suitor of Lana Turner, whose surprisingly solid performance as a showgirl on the skids was the best thing about *Ziegfeld Girl* (1941). With some ripe ensemble numbers, the film was essentially an MGM Christmas tree pegged on three careers: Judy Garland, good little girl, Hedy Lamarr, faithful wife, and Miss Turner, the skidder who couldn't take success. With little to do, Jimmy held his own.

He still held that Oscar. And on March 22, 1941, James Stewart became the first prominent Hollywood actor to be drafted into the United States Army, reportedly almost over the dead body of his boss, Louis B. Mayer.

It was an occasion, duly recorded in a revealing departure photograph that received wide circulation, showing Stewart standing before a train at the Los Angeles station, flanked by Mayer (looking rather quizzically benevolent), other members of the studio hierarchy and a cluster of top stars, among them Jeanette MacDonald, Clark Gable and Myrna Loy. It was an impressive "family" send-off and picture.

Stewart's war record was distinguished. Today he speaks of it noncommittally. Entering the Air Corps as a private, he became a bomber pilot and participated in twenty missions over Germany. In the service of his country, James Maitland Stewart was discovered to possess another facet of talent: genuine executive ability. He rose to the rank of full colonel, eventually becoming a brigadier general in the Air Force Reserve, retiring in 1968.

Four years—four war years of first-hand experience—give a man, an actor, time to think. Stewart had, obviously. His MGM contract had expired during his tenure of service. He returned to Hollywood not at his old Alma Mater but aligned with Liberty Films, one of the first independent filmmaking organizations, set up by George Stevens and Frank Capra, who had piloted *Mr. Smith Goes to Washington*. The kick-off project was *It's a Wonderful Life* (1946), with Capra directing, from a screenplay by Frances Goodrich, Albert Hackett (seasoned writers who later dramatized *The Diary of Anne Frank*) and Capra.

This quaintly warm parable, about virtue being its own reward, hovered sentimentally over a small-town family man beset with pressures and saved from suicide by a guardian angel. (He—and we—also see what would have happened if he *had* committed suicide.) With good work by Donna Reed, Lionel Barrymore, Thomas Mitchell and others, the film was as appealing as it was obvious. Stewart, in such a role, was excellent; there was no mistaking the intensity and sincerity of his feeling. Away from the camera, Stewart's eyes had seen more; they now showed more. The actor to this day calls it his favorite film of all. So does Capra.

This time the director went all out to depict the essence of the

A WIFE AND OTHER EVENTS

"wonderful life" as family, friends and honest work. As George Bailey, Stewart was a dreamer and armchair traveler managing a small business and driven to try suicide by a greedy banker, Barrymore. The hero's salvation was a heavenly messenger (Henry Travers) who showed Stewart how much bleaker the town would be without him. Stewart is finally restored to reality, his friends helpfully rallying around him.

Capra uses flashbacks to depict Stewart's boyhood and his courtship of Miss Reed, whose warm and open graciousness brings an extra glow to the movie. Barrymore comes over like Scrooge, however, and Travers' portrayal of the messenger from above is overly coy and sugary. But Beulah Bondi, H.B. Warner, Samuel S. Hinds and others in Capra's authoritative gallery of small-town types are fine.

Then came a mistake for Stewart—a film in which small-town Americana backfired rather awkwardly. This was *Magic Town* (1947) co-starring Jane Wyman, in an independent project by Robert Riskin (formerly a Capra writer), under William Wellman's direction. Stewart's folksy, drawling,

IT'S A WONDERFUL LIFE (1946).
With Donna Reed

IT'S A WONDERFUL LIFE (1946). With family and friends

comfortable approach didn't mesh with his role of a city-slicker public pollster who comes upon a small town which is a perfect composite of the United States. Neither did the tangled plot, nor the film's use of clichés, sentimentality and theatricality. As a seemingly good-natured satire, it turned into a sticky, thick piece of goods.

Stewart's next film, *A Miracle Can Happen* (1948) later retitled *On Our Merry Way*, was no better. This United Artists release was a silly, listless mess—an episodic, "all-star" grab-bag of comedy sketches involving Burgess Meredith, Paulette Goddard, Fred MacMurray and Dorothy Lamour. Stewart and Henry Fonda, his old friend, were best as a couple of beat-up musicians involved in a music contest at a California beach resort. Dropping all restraint, they simply indulged in some contagious, low-comedy mugging and slapstick. Stewart emerged from this jape unscathed. Nobody took it seriously, except perhaps the theater owners, mindful of short lines at the box office.

Call Northside 777 (1948), for

20th Century-Fox, gave Stewart a much needed success. This was the actor's ninth role as a journalist, a Chicago reporter convinced of a felon's innocence in a closed murder case who stubbornly dug in, going back through newspaper files and raking up and sifting evidence, and cleared his man (Richard Conte). In addition to a fine performance by Stewart, and a thoroughly credible one by the victimized Conte, there was convincing work by Lee J. Cobb, Helen Walker and Betty Garde. Henry Hathaway's crisp direction and the screenplay by James Cady and Jay Dratler helped to project a semidocumentary flavoring that lent authenticity and real suspense toward the end,

when the dogged, snooping reporter finally believes he can clear the wrongly convicted man.

The actual, pinpointed evidence that does clear him seems a bit far-fetched. With a howl of triumph, Stewart has magnified the background of a key photograph to establish a date matching the headline of a newspaper being hawked by a newsboy. This minuscule evidence probably did clear the convict and confirm his alibi in real life, since the picture was based on a supposedly true article by James P. McGuire. In any case, the drama and its crescendo of suspense make thoroughly engrossing viewing.

Rope (1948) was a most curious failure; the three subsequent thril-

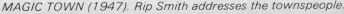

MAGIC TOWN (1947). Rip Smith addresses the townspeople.

A MIRACLE CAN HAPPEN (ON OUR MERRY WAY) (1948).
With Henry Fonda

lers that Stewart would make with Alfred Hitchcock were to establish him as the master's quintessential, all-American protagonist. But in *Rope*, both of them and a respectable cast, floundered in an earnest but self-conscious try for something different. In this Warners release about a cold-blooded "thrill" murder by two strange young men, Hitchcock used a stunt that proved tedious, even uncinematic. This was to literally recreate Patrick Hamilton's one-set play, *Rope's End*, confining the action to one room, in strict continuation of the story, with a flexible camera strategically exploring the room as an eavesdropping observer.

Kept in hard, static focus by the photography, as Hitchcock loud-pedaled the macabre aspect of a cocktail party with a corpse concealed in a chest, the performances themselves also seemed claustrophobic. Stewart offered a dour portrait of the two youths' friendly ex-teacher who sniffs out the Leopold-and-Loeb deed of John Dall and Farley Granger. Other party guests such as Joan Chandler, Constance Collier and Sir Cedric Hardwicke did well enough within the same confines. *Rope* may have taught Hitchcock something of a lesson, for every picture he has since made has been kept opened up as a motion picture; the stagelike

CALL NORTHSIDE 777 (1948). With Lee J. Cobb

ROPE (1948). With John Dall

confinement of *Dial M For Murder* at least was camouflaged in movie terms.*

Referring to the movie's unbroken time span of sustained, continuous action, François Truffaut, the French director and former film critic, insisted in a talk with Hitchcock that the idea of *Rope* remained admirable, viewed in the context of

Hitchcock's whole career. Truffaut added that "The classical cutting techniques ... have stood the test of time and still prevail today. Don't you agree?"

Hitchcock replied: "No doubt about it; films must be cut. As an experiment, *Rope* may be forgiven."** The director also recalled that the picture drew "good notices" but they were actually mixed. Hitchcock, in noting the

*Rope was innovative in several other ways. It was the first film Hitchcock produced and his first experiment in color, which he later used much more effectively in *Rear Window* (1954).

**François Truffaut, *Hitchcock*, (Simon and Schuster, New York, 1967), p. 134.

film's budget ("about $1,500,000"), said that Stewart's salary alone came to $300,000, a good indication of the actor's prestige at this point in his career and undoubtedly partial compensation for an interesting failure.

Coming after *Rope*, a breezy, genial comedy like *You Gotta Stay Happy* (1948) was a wise move for Stewart. No arch, drawn-out chitchat about death here; the aim was simply chucklesome diversion. Stewart was an ex-Army pilot operating a minor air-freight line

with a buddy, Eddie Albert. Heiress Joan Fontaine, fleeing a stuffy fiancé, hitches a ride with the boys and the rest is predictable. The three leads were natural and disarming, as were Roland Young, Willard Parker and especially Percy Kilbride as an Oklahoma farmer. So were Karl Tunberg's screenplay and H.C. Potter's direction of this amusing caper, released by Universal-International.

For two reasons 1949 was a momentous year for James Stewart. He made one of his finest films, *The*

ROPE (1948). With John Dall and Farley Granger

YOU GOTTA STAY HAPPY (1948). With Joan Fontaine

Stratton Story. And he took a wife.

Most men, if they marry at all, do so well before the age of forty. Hollywood stars were expected to wed well before that, especially someone as prominent as Stewart. Here he was, at the age of forty-one, apparently a confirmed bachelor, with a flourishing career. He was to be among the top ten box-office draws throughout the 1950s.

Off the screen, Stewart had not exactly been idle over the years. Since his arrival in the film colony, he had been active on the social scene. An early rumor had him

With wife Gloria at premiere

THE STRATTON STORY
(1949). As Monty Stratton

strongly infatuated with Margaret Sullavan, his old friend from the Falmouth stock company days. Stewart admitted an interest in Ginger Rogers. He had been a popular escort of such movie queens as Lana Turner, Jeanette MacDonald, Virginia Bruce, Alice Faye and Olivia de Havilland (whom he squired to the New York premiere of *Gone With the Wind*). Women seemed to like and trust him instinctively, on the set and off. To this day he is supposed to be using a gift from his old friend, Rosalind Russell—an expensive binder—for his "Hawkins" scripts. The forty-one-year-old actor had bided his time, matrimonially. Then it was high time.

In 1949, Stewart was married to the former Gloria Hatrich McLean, a vivacious nonprofessional, reportedly ten years the actor's junior, with two small sons by her previous marriage, Mike and Ronald (later a Marine First Lieutenant who was killed in Vietnam). The couple were to have twin daughters of their own, Kelly and Judy. A warm, outgoing and good-natured woman and an ideal counterpart to her shy, introverted husband, Gloria Stewart was almost immediately deemed by the sharp-eyed film colony to be exactly what Stewart needed. Twenty-five years later they are still together, with the actor's wife smoothly running their comfortable Beverly Hills mansion. Gloria Stewart is one of the best-liked of all Hollywood wives, a ticklish role in itself.

The year of their marriage also marked one of Stewart's biggest hits, *The Stratton Story*, with Stewart returning to MGM as Monty Stratton, the Chicago White Sox pitcher whose bright future was tragically darkened by a hunting accident in 1938. The film was tasteful, heart-tugging drama, from a beautifully understated screenplay by Douglas Morrow and Guy Trosper. Equally imaginative and honest was the direction of Sam Wood, who saw to it that the picture was touching but never treacly. As the brave, gritty protagonist surmounting the loss of a leg, Stewart was superb, fully projecting the despair and hopelessness of a baseball-diamond athlete abruptly rendered "half a man" yet manfully grappling for emotional strength to face up to the reality of his dilemma.

In one of the memorable dramatic moments of Hollywood films about sports figures (comparable to Gary Cooper's stadium farewell, as Lou Gehrig, in *Pride of the Yankees*), Stewart is first shown walking with his new wooden leg. We see him, grimly surrendering pride and mastering shame, as he slowly stands, unaided, and carefully teeters across his yard at home, back to the camera, grasping the tiny fingers of his small son who is just

THE STRATTON STORY (1949). With June Allyson

learning to walk for the first time. The two figures, tall and short, inch into the background, unforgettably.

Excellent performances also came from June Allyson as Stratton's wife, Frank Morgan and Agnes Moorehead. Miss Allyson reportedly made off with the front door-knob of the studio's Stratton home façade as a fond souvenir of the movie.

Of the three films in which Stewart portrayed famous Americans, the Stratton drama was the most effective.

With *Malaya* (1950), the actor started what might be called his ripest decade of screen appearances. Since he was no longer young, Stewart's romantic, leading-man roles began tapering off, mixed with more character portrayals such as the films that found him to be exceedingly at home on the range. In the suspense genre, he made three excellent Hitchcock films. The public obviously liked what it saw of Stewart in the 1950s, with the actor now among the first ten box-office champions during the entire decade.

The truth of the matter was that Stewart was aging gracefully, though on a somewhat zigzag career line, before our eyes, with character acting gradually taking over a career that never held one whit of glamour. Aesthetically, Stewart was biting in sharper and deeper. He was acting his age, while other stars around him were still clinging to vestiges of a young-buck image. Clark Gable was pursuing Grace Kelly in *Mogambo* with shiny false teeth and jet-dyed hair; he went out, panting for youthful Marilyn Monroe in *The Misfits*. In *Love in the Afternoon*, Gary Cooper was courting Audrey Hepburn, who was young enough to be his grand-daughter. But as his career moved into the 1950s, Stewart performed comfortably in mostly suitable roles. His initial three movies in this

STEWART IN THE FIFTIES: THE MELLOW YEARS

span were acceptable vehicles that did him neither harm nor good.

In *Malaya* (1950), a glossy-edged but sensibly devised adventure drama hinging on the United States' crucial, wartime need of raw rubber, Stewart was a journalist type (yes, again) officially recruited to help a worldly ex-convict, Spencer Tracy, infiltrate Japanese-held territory and spirit away a large supply from uneasy planters. This time Stewart played second-fiddle to Tracy, an older star, who not only had the meatier role, but also got the girl, Valentina Cortese. The final chapter was the best part of the film, a tense, gutsy section well directed by Richard Thorpe and colorfully evocative of the exotic locale, as the two men outwitted Japanese soldiers and bullied the planters into cooperation.

Most of the time Stewart loped around, dour and suspicious, in Tracy's wake; the effect was credible and nicely cynical. Tracy was familiarly Tracy, sturdy and reliable. Miss Cortese, in her curious West Coast exposure to movies, as usual did better by Hollywood than it did by her. There were effective sideline rumblings from Sydney Greenstreet and Lionel Barrymore.

MALAYA (1950). With Spencer Tracy and Lester Matthews

Shelley Winters was flamboyantly on view in Anthony Mann's *Winchester .73* (1950) but this was one Western where the hero, for a change, was more interested in his gun, the title one. As Stewart kept recapturing his Winchester, while it shifted hands, the picture moved forward in lively, broad fashion as a lightly tongue-in-cheek adventure not to be taken too seriously. At times Stewart amusingly suggested his role in *Destry Rides Again*. Helpful flanking came from Dan Duryea, Stephen McNally, John McIntyre and Millard Mitchell.

In *Broken Arrow* (1950), Stewart came off none too well as a spunky Civil War veteran supporting a tribe of Southwest Apaches against some dastardly whites. This time Stewart's fumbling, slow gestures and drawl seemed strangely at odds with the film's altruistic aim—to dignify the American Indian on the screen, for a change. Nor was Stewart, so much older, convincing in his love scenes with youthful Debra Paget, as an Indian maiden. (Stewart lost the girl here for reason enough: she's murdered by nasty

73

WINCHESTER .73 (1950). As Lin McAdam

BROKEN ARROW (1950). With Jeff Chandler, Debra Paget, and Lee McGregor

whites.) Jeff Chandler's Cochise looked fine, but his Indian chief behaved too nobly and spoke too articulately.

Yet the film's underlying, earnest tone of justice and decency about Indians put it across and Stewart, rather awkwardly, with it. But it was far from a personal triumph. Because of either Delmer Daves' direction or the actor's own conception of his role, Stewart seemed uneasy.

The actor's luck changed with the next three projects. *The Jackpot* (1950), made at Fox, was a brightly funny and lightly scathing takeoff on the woes and tribulations besetting a top winner of one of those glib, giveaway radio shows. The joy for the winner, Stewart, turned into chaos. Overshadowing his deluge of prizes was the specter of an enormous income-tax bite.

The film was consistently amusing and entertaining, with the spontaneous work of Stewart as the mesmerized protagonist, Barbara

THE JACKPOT (1950). With James Gleason

Hale as his wife and a score of expert supporting players such as Fred Clark, James Gleason and Alan Mowbray; Walter Lang's easy, sporting direction, and the screenplay which Phoebe and Henry Ephron deftly derived from John McNulty's true-life article in *The New Yorker*.

Mary C. Chase may have pulled a rabbit—a 6-foot, 3½-inch one—out of her playwright's hat for the prize-winning *Harvey*, a successful Broadway comedy in 1944. But it was Stewart, repeating the original Frank Fay role in the 1950 movie at Universal-International, who pulled audiences closer than ever to the heart and spirit of the play with an endearingly wistful portrait of the whimsical, imaginative alcoholic, Elwood P. Dowd. Rather surprisingly, the movie version added a dimension, a sweetness and perhaps even a kind of credibility that the play did not have, and Stewart's performance had much to do with it.

Mrs. Chase and Oscar Brodney wrote a most sensible movie adaptation and the supporting cast was exceptionally appealing, starting, of

HARVEY (1950). With Josephine Hull

HARVEY (1950). With Peggy Dow and Charles Drake

course, with that inimitable old darling from Broadway, Josephine Hull, as the hero's sister, and including Victoria Horne and Jesse White (also from the stage version), Cecil Kellaway, William Lynn, Peggy Dow and Charles Drake. As touching and amusing as Frank Fay's original performance was, Stewart's work on the screen somehow added a more personal, meaningful glow.

Harvey has been a kind of vest-pocket career-within-a-career for Stewart. In 1947, a year when he made only one film, the less than magical *Magic Town*, he had accepted an offer to return to the Broadway stage as a summer replacement for Fay in the Chase comedy, which won the Pulitzer Prize. This was the postwar era and Stewart, though definitely a movie name, was not the powerhouse star

*NO HIGHWAY IN THE SKY (1951). With Ronald Squire and Jack Hawkins
(most prominent in background)*

he was to become. His stage return drew good notices, to no particular blaring of publicity trumpets; Stewart subsequently replaced Fay as the star of the show, but his real star still rose in the West.

Three years later, the film version of *Harvey* won Stewart his fourth Oscar nomination. Then exactly twenty years later, co-starring with Helen Hayes, he essayed *Harvey* on Broadway once more, a triumphant revival that brought Stewart high personal acclaim that could not have been more welcome or reassuring to a Broadway alumnus turned major movie commodity. The *New York Daily News* put it simply: "He is offering a master class in acting with each performance." *The New York Times* declared: "(This) production of *Harvey* restores James Stewart and a sense of innocence to the American theater. As Elwood, (Stewart's) garrulous, gentle, genial presence is a delight."

Typically, perhaps, and certainly becomingly, Stewart had gone to his hotel after the opening-night performance for a good night's sleep. He and his wife hadn't seen fit to wait up until the wee hours for the reviews; perhaps the Stewarts simply didn't care about undergoing the sophisticated East Coast ritual of waiting up for the newspapers. Nor had they read the reviews by midmorning, when a friend telephoned congratulations.

Why had Stewart elected to return to Broadway at that time? He told the Sunday *Times** that he and Mrs. Stewart "kind of welcomed the change. We found ourselves sitting around Beverly Hills having conversations with our two dogs." Stewart found Hollywood "a little quiet and depressing right now." The actor said that he had always loved the play and wanted to do it again, at a more appropriate age. He wasn't particularly satisfied with the movie version or his performance in it, he added.

Whatever Stewart's retrospective opinion, *Harvey* remains one of the outstanding films the actor made during the span of the 1950s. Most of his other fifties films were also a step forward—some of them may be considered time-killers; none did him any noticeable harm. And on the heels of the screen *Harvey* came one of the most quietly beguiling pictures Stewart ever made, *No Highway in the Sky* (1951).

An odd title. And it usually takes people considerable pause to link it to Stewart—or for that matter to his co-stars, Marlene Dietrich and Glynis Johns. Another minute is required to recall what this movie was all about. It was a Fox drama, made in England, with Stewart playing a

*February 22, 1970

80

THE GREATEST SHOW ON EARTH (1952). With Betty Hutton

THE GREATEST SHOW
ON EARTH (1952).
As "Buttons"

BEND OF THE RIVER (1952). With Rock Hudson, J.C. Flippen, and Julia Adams

mousy, widowed mathematician aboard a transatlantic flight who becomes so alarmed over the structural weakness of the new model of plane (he has done some frantic, midair figuring on paper) that he disables the plane during a stopover to keep it from resuming flight. Stewart's fears have already been sympathetically heard by Miss Dietrich, as a chic actress, and Miss Johns, as a stewardess. Both return to England to help Stewart fight a lunacy charge.

Not the juiciest of plot pegs, granted. But this adaptation of a novel by Nevil Shute was original, it was nicely paced by Henry Koster's direction and it was skillfully played by Stewart and the others. The dialogue was excellent in the screenplay by R.C. Sherriff, Oscar Millard and Alec Coppel. The most telling critical comment was made by Bosley Crowther in *The New York Times*: "Although there is nothing conspicuously explosive about the picture, it grows upon you as it goes along."

At this point in his career, Stewart's face and expression no longer reflected the youthful idealism of a *Destry* or a *Mr. Smith* or, more acerbically, a Philadelphia" journalist; or, for that matter, a gentle Elwood P. Dowd. In the demeanor, looks and behavior of the hero of *No Highway In the Sky*, there is a new, settled maturity without resignation, a kind of intelligent acceptance. The Stewart trademark—the casual, homespun fumbling—is no longer dominant, but shifted to the fringes. Here is a beautifully, deftly chiseled performance that hardly seems to be acting at all.

Stewart's trademarked fumbling was to swing back, often front and center, to critical carping (understandably) in lesser vehicles, especially in the 1960s, when the Stewart films became fewer and farther between. But now, early in the 1950s, this was the becomingly mellowed, personal imprint on the screen of a successful, newly married, forty-three-year-old Hollywood actor, moving steadily toward his peak, the 1959 *Anatomy of a Murder*. It would be five years before Alfred Hitchcock would draw upon this maturing image for *Rear Window*, the first of three Stewart-Hitchcock hits that made the actor's career catch fire on a new level—suspense. Meanwhile, after *No Highway*, Stewart made a shrewd move in joining Cecil B. DeMille's *The Greatest Show On Earth* (1952).

This particular *Greatest Show* was a long distance from cinematic art, but it was an immensely entertaining extravaganza, with the master of spectacle (some call it lard) cleverly juggling a plot of sorts, a sizable roundup of star names (Charlton Heston and Betty Hutton had the most footage) and all that could visually be squeezed from and poured back into a big-top performance. Stewart's role was lean but catching, that of a mystery clown, never seen without full facial makeup, who turns out to be a fugitive from justice. Stewart was on display here in the biggest moneymaker of the year, which also won veteran director DeMille an Oscar at long last.

As undemanding, color-splashed entertainment, the movie cannot be faulted. In its superb photography evoking the mammoth display perennially staged by the Ringling Brothers and Barnum & Bailey unit and in a welter of subplots crammed into the story, the movie certainly surpassed any previous circus package put on the screen. Taken as a romance, rather than a genuine drama of circus life, the Fredric M. Frank-Barré Lyndon-Theodore St. John screenplay was busily acceptable, with Heston as the circus boss with sawdust in his blood, Miss Hutton as his aerialist sweetheart, Cornel Wilde as her handsome, daredevil partner, Stewart as the

THE NAKED SPUR (1953). With Janet Leigh

enigmatic clown, Lyle Bettger as a wily elephant trainer, Gloria Grahame as his selfish girl and Dorothy Lamour as a decorative show ornament.

Very solidly, the movie captured the complicated juggernaut movement of the circus troupe and its setting-up arrival for a performance. Topping it all, like a huge, explosive cherry on a dessert, De-Mille added a climactic train wreck that spilled across the screen, animals included. It may not have been art, but *The Greatest Show On Earth* was not dull.

Universal's *Bend of the River* (1952) and MGM's *The Naked Spur* (1953) displayed a tough and even tougher Stewart. Here was good, solid trouping with no Western nonsense, either from Stewart or the two films. What the first one came down to (Anthony Mann directed both) was a territorial conflict between farmers and miners, with Stewart as a frontiersman leading a band of Oregon-bound pioneers and Arthur Kennedy as a roughneck who joins the miners. Both actors gave strong performances in a neatly constructed movie.

The second film centered on a taut, scroungy manhunt and its aftermath, knotting together on the trail a group of less-than-saintly denizens, from Stewart, as a frankly opportunist reward-seeker of no particular conscience, to

Robert Ryan, the villainous quarry, and Janet Leigh, as a thawing spitfire. Ralph Meeker and Millard Mitchell did well here, too.

But MGM's *Carbine Williams* (1952) missed out and so did Stewart, as a Tarheel convict at a prison farm who is finally pardoned and released—after proving his noble character—for inventing a brand-new method for operating guns. This was a strangely unconvincing movie that seemed dramatically stacked, with a pat, artificial flavor and a wavering set of values. Stewart was affecting enough, but punctuated his performance with insistent gulping and fumbling; Wendell Corey was a bit more believable as the warden.

Stewart hit an outright clinker with *Thunder Bay* (1953), an adventure geographically straddling the Gulf of Mexico oil lands and a shrimp bed. This was standard moviemaking, routinely directed by Anthony Mann, about a troupe of wildcatters striking for oil and their involvement with Cajun shrimp fishermen. Stewart and such worthies as Dan Duryea and Gilbert Roland handled flat material squarely, valiantly and hopelessly.

Thunder Bay was best forgotten. Stewart could shrug it off since Universal had paged him for *The Glenn Miller Story* (1954).

This was an eminently satisfactory film, from Stewart's convincing

CARBINE WILLIAMS (1952). With Wendell Corey

depiction of the famous bandleader, firmly enhanced by June Allyson as his wife (from *The Stratton Story*) to a good Valentine Davies-Oscar Brodney script that followed the musician's career rise to his wartime disappearance on a military plane. This was not gutsy drama, but a reasonable biography, under Anthony Mann's balanced direction, with the story arranged in warmly sentimental, human terms. The sound track was a disarming bonanza of Miller music, especially appealing amidst the blast of cacophonic music in the mid-1950's and Stewart simulated (to Joe Yuki's dubbing) the trombone playing of Miller surprisingly well. Though faked, the actor's playing seemed assured and professional, in contrast to his musical diddling with Fonda in *A Miracle Can Happen* back in 1948 and that hoarsely wistful chanting of "Easy to Love" many years earlier in Cole Porter's *Born to Dance*.

Word filtered East during the *Glenn Miller* production that Stewart was "giving the studio trouble." This can be taken with a barrel of salt; Hollywood being what is is, it may even have been the other way around. But it was one of the rare times that such a rumor persisted about an actor with a reputation for professional behavior and a realistic deliver-the-goods-attitude commensurate with the arrangements of each assignment—certain project approvals and a specified salary—fulfulled on a business level.

The Glenn Miller Story was another attractive feather for his cap in Stewart's trio of screen biographies of famous Americans. The movie lacked the intelligently reflected profundity of *The Stratton Story*. It certainly lacked the dramatic thrust and tingling symbolism of *The Spirit of St. Louis* (Lindbergh). But the actor's portrayal of Miller and the frame of the picture made it one of the most winning show-business stories since James Cagney's George M. Cohan in *Yankee Doodle Dandy*.

Five years later, in 1957, Stewart ran into air trouble on two levels. The careful, workmanlike movie adaptation of Charles A. Lindbergh's autobiographical account of his milestone, solo flight across the Atlantic, as provocative a role as Stewart had ever undertaken, simply was not the powerhouse intended. That same year, after the Warners project was released, there was an imbroglio on Capitol Hill, about what should have been immediate approval of the promotion of Col. James Stewart to brigadier general by the Senate Armed Services Committee.

Stewart's promotion was challenged and blocked by Senator Margaret Chase Smith until the

THE GLENN MILLER STORY (1954). As Glenn Miller

THE GLENN MILLER STORY (1954). With June Allyson

matter was settled in his favor two years later. The senator from Maine charged that the Air Force, in the matter of reserve-officer advancements, was putting "success in big business and the movies" above actual military training. Throughout the awkward publicity, as the hassle dragged on and on, Stewart typically remained silent.

In The Spirit of St. Louis, Stewart's boyish demeanor and angular quietude physically suggested the famed "Lone Eagle," but unfortunately he came across as the familiar type of awkward, likable hero filmgoers had seen many times before. The screenplay, written by Wendell Mayes and director Billy Wilder, dealt only superficially with Lindbergh's background. The drama ended abruptly with the plane's landing at Le Bourget airport, suggesting the end of an adventure more than a towering, historical accomplishment. But to

THE SPIRIT OF ST. LOUIS (1957). As Charles A. Lindbergh

many viewers, the film's antiseptic emotional quality was inevitable in a drama that excluded the heart-wrenching, personal tragedy of the kidnaping of Lindbergh's infant son.

"We should have done the whole story," Wilder ruefully conceded later. There was, however, one evocative aspect to this disappointing film: an exceptionally stirring score by Franz Waxman. Tony Thomas had this to say about it: "The film needed a score that would support the bare dramatics of a man flying the Atlantic alone—the loneliness and the apprehension he must have felt on that pioneering flight. Waxman's music carries the burden; it literally accompanies the lonely aviator and speaks his mind as he looks down at the ocean and the various lands over which he flies. The music also alludes to the danger of drowsiness, his fear of not being able to land the plane, and his prayers. Truly a landmark in film scoring."*

*Tony Thomas, *Music For the Movies* (A.S. Barnes and Tanqueray., Inc., 1973, New York and London), p. 89.

THE SPIRIT OF ST. LOUIS (1957). With director Billy Wilder

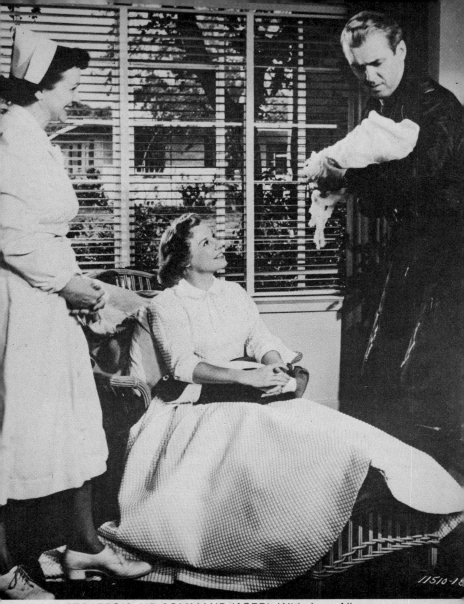

STRATEGIC AIR COMMAND (1955). With June Allyson

THE FAR COUNTRY (1955). With Walter Brennan

As a Stewart vehicle, *The Spirit of St. Louis* had had an aviation forerunner two years earlier in Paramount's *Strategic Air Command* (1955), the kind of title that usually prompts an indifferent shrug. Yet it was not a bad film, despite such frayed material as an eye-popping, sky-blackening swarm of Air Force planes in spectacular evidence— a massive propaganda poster on high—and a tired plot line which offered Stewart and his perennial movie wife, June Allyson, as a baseball player called back into service and his helpful spouse. For all the clichés, the ground drama had an aura of good-natured conviction. Stewart and Miss Allyson were quite good indeed and Anthony Mann's direction was smoothly professional.

We come now to the trio of Alfred Hitchcock thrillers, *Rear Window* (1954), *The Man Who Knew Too Much* (1956) and *Vertigo* (1958), which not only enhanced the actor's career lustrously—to a healthy jingle of box-office coins—but merge in retrospect, not only as beguiling suspense variations by a master, but also as a magnetic flow of reactions by an antithetical American hero type (which Stewart had become) caught in a puzzling quandary.

The three films were so effective and Stewart so good that a spate of perfectly respectable Westerns the actor made at this time are inconsequential. These are Universal's *The* *Far Country* (1955), a scenic caper with Stewart and such veterans as Walter Brennan and John McIntire giving familiar material a rough but adult going over; Columbia's *The Man From Laramie* (1955), an even tougher yarn, with Stewart taking on an entire Apache-country town to avenge his murdered brother; and Universal's *Night Passage* (1957), best described as a railroad Western, with Stewart's taut, cutting performance providing real dimension.

Of the Hitchcock trio, Para-

REAR WINDOW (1954). With Grace Kelly

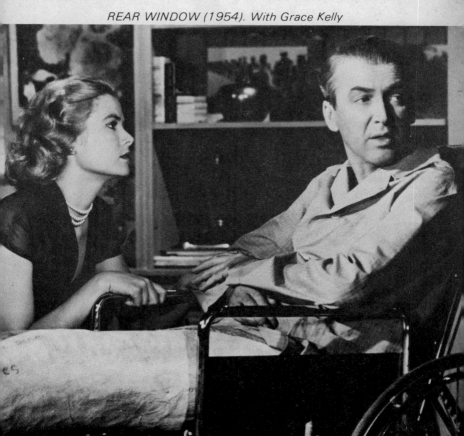

REAR WINDOW (1954). With Thelma Ritter

mount's *Rear Window* was the first and best. With a clever, precise script by John Michael Hayes, developed from a story by Cornell Woolrich, Hitchcock had himself a cinematic field day, opening up the material like a shrewd Peeping Tom as the camera scanned fragments of activity and lives in a jumbled Greenwich Village courtyard. The viewpoint was that of Stewart, as an inquisitive news photographer with a broken leg, propped in a casement near his wheelchair and alerted to action, with binoculars, when he suspects a sullen salesman (Raymond Burr), seen through a window slit, of butchering his wife.

Drifting in at Stewart's elbow, as his determined curiosity mounted, were Grace Kelly as his chic fiancée-model, Thelma Ritter as an earthy nurse, and Wendell Corey as a professional sleuth, all of them quite good. Pegged on plain curiosity and nosiness, the movie's tone was nicely balanced by the lifelike, often wry dialogue and broadened as Hitchcock's camera touched on urban loneliness and isolation in its kaleidoscopic scanning of the courtyard.

But it was Hitchcock's richly detailed crescendo of suspense, his stunning use of color photography, and the steady penetration of Stewart's central performance, played from the wheelchair, that brought in the movie as a high-grade thriller.

For all the picture's tone of detachment, as Stewart (and the camera) study the signs of surrounding life visible in the rear courtyard, the film also has an appealing, marginal compassion and understanding as we glimpse a wistful spinster, a pair of preoccupied newlyweds, a bachelor musician, a sprightly, half-clad dancer and a childless couple out with a dog. One of the most affecting moments in the movie is the wife's discovery that the dog has eaten poison and her accusing wail to the courtyard— "Why? Why would anybody want to kill a little dog?"—with everybody drawn to a window except Burr, the killer, who is seen smoking in the dark.

The climax of *Rear Window* was highly suspenseful, with Burr finally on to Stewart's furtive plan to trap him, entering Stewart's room and attacking him while blinded by defensive flashbulbs.

Stewart was even better in Paramount's *The Man Who Knew Too Much*, a worthy but somewhat lesser teaser that Hitchcock had already filmed a bit more compactly in 1934 in England without the splash of color photography and the exotic background of the Morocco-made opening. Still, it was good, solid, tourist-class Hitchcock. Stewart was superb in a characterization of greater psychological depth than *Rear Window*, as a pleasant American sightseer in Marrakesh with his wife, Doris Day, and a young son, Christopher Olsen, who hears the mumblings of a murdered stranger, finds his boy has been kidnaped by spies as a hostage for the information, and finally corners them in London. Here again the climax was unadulterated Hitchcockian suspense: a desperate, last-second foiling of an attempted assassination in a crowded concert hall.

Miss Day, Brenda de Banzie, Bernard Miles and the others were first-rate, but Stewart's portrait of a decent, average citizen transformed into a seething, independent lion of outraged courage—while coolly keeping the protocol-minded police in line—was something to behold.

And so was his work in Paramount's *Vertigo*, an intricate blend of sustained bafflement and infatuation that is more provocative now, on television, than it was originally, with the actor as an ex-detective suffering from acrophobia (fear of heights) who is hired by a San Francisco magnate to shadow his moody, wandering wife, Kim Novak.

Here Hitchcock used the color camera like a tantalizing palette to capture the dazzling picturesque-

THE MAN WHO KNEW TOO MUCH (1956). With Christopher Olsen and Bernard Miles

VERTIGO (1958). With Kim Novak

ANATOMY OF A MURDER (1959). With Eve Arden and Arthur O'Connell

ness of the city, and also to inch forward the complex plot. The story was extremely devious, derived from a tale by the French authors who originated *Diabolique*, and it loops and twists cunningly as the hero, falling in love with the enigmatic woman he is stalking, fails to prevent her suicide, stumbles upon her exact look-alike (apparently) and this time bird-dogs her trail to a tragic end.

The film is still not entirely convincing; there is one serious snag in the last reel. See for yourself. For once, at least in drama, Miss Novak's off-into-space staring suited her role as a woman of mystery. But Stewart's mercurial shifts

of expression—disbelief, bewilderment, desire and determination —were an ideal mirror of reactions for such a Hitchcock hoax. The performance of the actor, with at least one foot on the ground, the use of color and a genuinely haunting score by Bernard Herrmann made *Vertigo* work as an intriguing spider-web thriller.

Stewart has called Hitchcock and John Ford his favorite directors. No one, whether actor, actress or crew technician, has ever been known to say this about Otto Preminger, a workman-like director whose best-known movie remains *Laura*. Traditionally, Preminger will neatly assemble a rather slick package of entertainment, people it with uncommonly good, colorful casts and then proceed to shout at and abuse the actors when the camera is about to roll. Such was the prospect when Stewart, Lee Remick, Ben Gazzara, Arthur O'Connell, George C. Scott, Kathryn Grant, Eve Arden and Brooks West, her husband, and a Columbia crew converged on two small towns in Michigan to film *Anatomy of a Murder*, which yielded perhaps James Stewart's best screen performance out of seventy-three—a long, varied track record for any actor.

It was an excellent drama, cleverly adapted by Wendell Mayes from Robert Traver's best-selling novel, a striking study of the personalities involved in a criminal trial. The picture brimmed with small-town authenticity and color and under Preminger's keen eye, it ultimately exploded in a long, detailed and fascinating courtroom showdown, the trial of a moody young Army lieutenant (Gazzara) for killing a man accused of raping his luscious, less-than-saintly wife (Miss Remick). The acting, the gallery of characters, the movie's realistic look (including a natural, ingratiating cameo by Boston's Judge Joseph N. Welch as the trial judge) and the impact of the trial itself, climaxed by a brilliant battle of attorneys between George C. Scott (prosecution) and Stewart (defense), all meshed memorably.

ANATOMY OF A MURDER (1959). With Eve Arden, Lee Remick, Ben Gazzara and Royal Beal

BELL, BOOK AND CANDLE (1958). With Kim Novak

Most penetrating of all was Stewart's acting, whether poking about the shady fringes of the community for new evidence, shaping his defense case with his colleagues, or mercilessly grilling witnesses on the stand. The film holds together well now despite flaws: there is an out-of-place, jazzy score by Duke Ellington that had nothing to do with the placid, unruffled look of the small community, and the case in question does seem a little over-cooked, certainly less than histori-cal. Also, the movie is too long at two hours and forty minutes.

Stewart's performance in *Anatomy of a Murder* in 1959 re-mains the crowning personal achievement during the ripest de-cade of his career. The previous year had brought *Bell, Book and Candle*, a pleasant bauble about modern witchcraft, co-starring his *Vertigo* leading lady, Kim Novak. Stewart was adequate, nothing more, in a role that amounted to his last appearance as a graying roman-tic lead; Miss Novak, always more at home in comedy than in drama, did well enough as a beautiful young witch. But the spice of this Colum-bia package, based on the play by John Van Druten, was contributed by the color styles of Eliot Elisofon and the spellbinding color photo-graphy by the veteran James Wong Howe. They gave the film an arrest-

THE F.B.I. STORY (1959). As Chip Hardesty

ing patina of occult make-believe, as the scenes shifted from the heroine's atelier for primitive art, to a smoky nightclub in Greenwich Village, and, magically tinted, to New York streets at dawn and twilight. The drollery of Jack Lemmon, Elsa Lanchester, Hermione Gingold and Ernie Kovacs was also helpful.

Stewart's final film portrait of the 1950's was that of a man combining warmth, earnestness, strength and charm. All these sterling features were embodied in Chip Hardesty, a dedicated government agent in Warners' *The F.B.I. Story* ((1959), directed by Mervyn LeRoy and co-starring Vera Miles as Hardesty's wife. This colorful, over-the-years saga efficiently equated a parade of heroic F.B.I. investigations with Stewart's personal activities in the story and with the (his) American family. The effect was patriotic and reassuring as the film blended in technical footage of the Bureau's technical facilities and operations, but it was a far cry from director LeRoy's primitive but powerful 1931 crime melodrama, *Little Caesar*.

Of the fifteen Stewart movies from 1960 to the present, his best work has been in Westerns. Today it seems rather peculiar reasoning on somebody's part that when the actor finally succumbed to television he elected to try a family situation-comedy series (a failure) that more or less extended the tone and antics of three lesser vehicles, *Mr. Hobbs Takes a Vacation, Take Her, She's Mine*, and *Dear Brigitte*. The reasoning, obviously, was that Stewart would be more effective on the home screen as an awkward, absent-minded bumbler. This was strange, considering the phenomenal popularity of such shoot-em-up series as *Bonanza, Have Gun, Will Travel* and *The Big Valley*. In any case, it is hard to fathom the bypassing of the actor's meat-and-potatoes, Western potential, radiating so strongly from *Two Rode Together, The Man Who Shot Liberty Valance, Cheyenne Autumn, The Rare Breed* and *Firecreek*.

Dotted in and around this impressive quintet were some pretty fair vehicles and some outright failures. Columbia's *The Mountain Road* (1960), for instance, found, according to *The New York Times*, "a real pro like Jimmy Stewart holding together a mild little war sermon," a World War II drama with the star heading a small American Army demolition team in the craggy Chinese back country. It

STEWART IN THE SIXTIES: MAINLY WESTERNS

was rather plodding, routine action fare, directed by Daniel Mann.

There was very little substance in *Mr. Hobbs Takes a Vacation* (1962), pairing Stewart and Maureen O'Hara, but it was at least a chipper family comedy, mainly due to the game performing and the general brightness of Nunnally Johnson's screenplay, as the sprawling all-American Hobbs tribe cluttered a freakish old house on the Pacific Coast.

Despite the familiar trappings, this movie has some funny moments. One of the most amusing occurs toward the beginning, when the family car pulls up for the first time at their vacation home on the beach, rented sight unseen. The family gape at it—the house is a gingerbread Gothic horror—as a sound-track organ, in a clever touch by director Henry Koster, formidably wheezes Bach. "It makes you think of Finland, doesn't it, Brenda?" says a determinedly cheerful Miss O'Hara to the back-seat servant, Minerva Urecal. "It's vurse," comes an answering growl. Miss Urecal, as the cook, figures in another bit of script brightness, when she threatens to leave because Stewart has "cursed at

THE MOUNTAIN ROAD (1960). With Glenn Corbett

her." The parents huddle, baffled. "All I said to her," Stewart tells his wife, "was—now for some sun on the beach." A light dawns; they both explode in laughter.

Johnson's genial screenplay obviously owed much to the source, a novel by Edward Streeter (*Father of the Bride*). There were pleasant supporting contributions by John McGiver, Marie Wilson and Reginald Gardiner, with Lauri Peters and Fabian heading up the assortment of young people and children.

MGM's *How the West Was Won* (1963) was a vast patchwork quilt of outdoor adventure vignettes, with a teeming cast, three directors (including the distinguished John Ford), a rather flat, strangely episodic script by James R. Webb and a whopping budget—all of it stretched out unimaginatively to fill a wide, Cinerama screen, running nearly three hours and revealing little or nothing of how the West was won. There were action-crammed sequences, such as a thundering buffalo stampede and an Indian attack. But the film, for all its size and

MR. HOBBS TAKES A VACATION (1962). With Maureen O'Hara

HOW THE WEST WAS WON (1963). Surviving pioneers hold
a funeral service.

expense, seldom suggested reality, let alone history. Stewart, as a fur trapper, was top-billed over Debbie Reynolds, Carroll Baker, Karl Malden, Agnes Moorehead, Gregory Peck, John Wayne, Richard Widmark, Henry Fonda, and many others.

During the filming I asked Stewart a question. We were both "on location" near Paducah, Kentucky; my assignment was an article on the first expensive Cinerama Western. We sat on a log close to the Ohio River. The entire company had been working since 5:00 A.M., sloshing through mud and climbing over rocks; they were now waiting for the sun to come out. Why, I wondered, should one of the most financially secure and famed of all Hollywood actors still be putting himself through this? The waiting itself was tedious and killing.

Stewart looked tired and worn. His coloring was pale behind the actor's coating of makeup, his buckskin shoulder-padding was obvious. Why, I said gently, did he keep at it like this?

I thought he wouldn't answer. Then: "Waaall, it's keeping busy. At what I know. It's a little money, too." Was audience response a kind of satisfaction? "Uh-huh. Sure. Hello, Aggie." We were joined by Miss Moorehead, a friendly, alert woman. "I heard that," she chirped, eyes twinkling. "That's the real reward. Maybe it's actor's ego. When I was touring last year for Paul Gregory, audiences in Cairo got my points just as quickly as those in New York." She snapped her fingers. "Like that."

Stewart nodded. "Speaking of

108

TAKE HER, SHE'S MINE (1963). With Sandra Dee

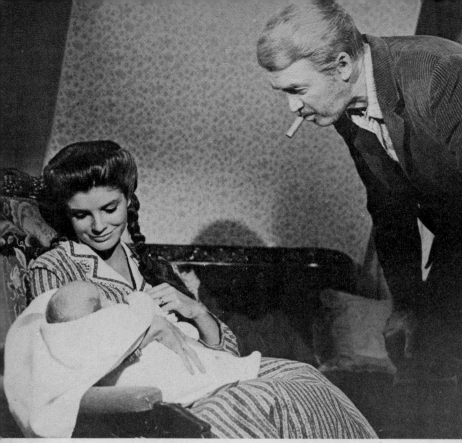

SHENANDOAH (1965). With Katharine Ross

money, I paid out a lot not long ago for my son to learn Spanish. When I took my family to Spain last year, one night in a restaurant he leaned across the table and said, *'Pasa el sal.'* That means pass the salt. That's all he got out of it—those lessons and that money. *'Pasa el sal!'* "

The actor's wry, mock indignation was that of any practical-minded father—not a rich Hollywood actor—who had wasted good money.

Stewart had a problem daughter, a screen one played by Sandra Dee, and a problem picture in *Take Her, She's Mine* (1963), a Fox frolic that went over like a lead balloon. This one, another Nunnally Johnson screenplay based on the stage com-

*THE FLIGHT
OF THE PHOENIX (1966).*
As Frank Towns

edy by Phoebe and Henry Ephron, scraped the barrel for laughs, and Stewart, as an harrassed father trailing his freethinking daughter to Paris, was awkwardly, unbecomingly trapped squarely in the middle of it. And *Dear Brigitte* (1965), another Fox release, wasn't much better as humor, with the actor as a tweedy, dry-spoken professor saddled with a genius son. The game cast included Glynis Johns, Fabian, little Billy Mumy, with a silly, wedged-in "cameo" by Brigitte Bardot, the French "sex kitten."

Universal's *Shenandoah* (1965) at least restored Stewart to provocative terrain, Civil War Virginia. As the tough-minded head of an isolationist farm clan, tragically drawn into the conflict, Stewart gave a good, tough-fibered performance that eventually softened with the screenplay, a commendably original one by James Lee Barrett. Andrew V. McLaglen's direction provided color and gripping portions but the final result was rambling and overly detailed.

It was bound to happen, at least to an actor who had personified the Strategic Air Command and the Lone Eagle (Lindbergh), let alone flown twenty bombing missions during World War II: a plane crash-survival drama. Such was *The Flight of the Phoenix* (1966), a Fox misfire directed by Robert Aldrich, it being mainly a tedious, over-drawn dispute over a makeshift plane (pieced together from the wreckage) between the pilot, Stewart, and a German, Hardy Kruger, under a blistering Sahara sun, as the other thirsty survivors bristled and collided among themselves.

"What's in it for me?"

This scornful query, echoed repeatedly by Stewart in John Ford's *Two Rode Together* (1961), pinpoints the character and the bluntly realistic performance of a now-veteran actor whose appearances in five Westerns, ranging from very good to towering, through 1968, crystallized a lasting image of a man more than at home on the range.

Stewart's image in the Western genre had been shaping and toughening up in such biting characterizations as the earthy heroes of *Bend of the River*, *The Naked Spur*, *The Man From Laramie* and *Night Passage*. But this later cluster of frontier vehicles (with other Stewart stints in between) bit deeper, harder and more memorably. With the exception of *The Man Who Shot Liberty Valance*, a good movie with Stewart more or less along for the ride in a reasonable performance that nevertheless suggested the fumbling idealist of yore, this quintet of range dramas nailed to the wall a lasting image of leathery maturity.

TWO RODE TOGETHER (1961). With Richard Widmark

The aging Stewart was not the still-handsome prairie dasher conveyed by Gary Cooper, nor did Stewart have the mercurial bluster of a Burt Lancaster, when this actor elected to straddle a horse; or the born-to-the-saddle hulkiness of a John Wayne. The ultimate effect of the James Stewart who emerges from this later gallery of Westerns is that of a wiry, cautious-footed beanpole, hat and clothes hanging loosely, of slow and barbed-wire plain talk and eyes that bore through as surely and methodically as acid.

The character he played in *Two Rode Together* is a good example. (Stewart was to work with Ford later in *How the West Was Won*; his sequence was far and away the best thing about this episodic stew, but it became lost in the wide-screen confusion and more or less spiraled down the drain.) In this Columbia release, co-starred with Richard Widmark, Stewart was finally teamed with a great Western director whose formidable reputation and technical prowess (starting with the landmark *Stagecoach*) brooked no interference, even from the studio. This time, as happened two years later, there was no over-the-shoulder hovering by MGM, anxious to fill up a wide screen with tired, million-dollar razzle-dazzle.

Superficially, *Two Rode Together*
was a typical Ford project, with a lean, taut screenplay which Frank Nugent had derived from a novel by Will Cook. In addition to Stewart and Widmark, the picture had the able supporting roundup traditional in a Ford Western. Ford's theme was a continuation of the subject of Indian prejudice explored in his earlier *The Searchers*, minus his usual panoramic background and holding closer to the story and performances.

Stewart, with top billing, played a flinty, tippling, frankly mercenary frontier sheriff commissioned to bring in a group of white captives Indians had spirited away years before and (in a powerful confrontation scene) no longer recognizable and even behaving like barbarians. Ford kept a tight, hard-hitting and unsentimental focus on the unraveling pathos and irony of the tragedy, as in the scene of the attempted lynching of a white boy, screaming that he is a Comanche after murdering the white woman who tries to rehabilitate him.

Widmark did well enough as a stalwart cavalry officer but his romance with the dewy-eyed Shirley Jones was the film's one standard compromise. The veteran actress, Mae Marsh and, briefly, Linda Cristal and others were also effective, but Stewart's realistic sheriff led the performances and it was one of the peaks of his long career.

Ironically, having achieved a masterly Western portrait of an antihero, Stewart's next role for Ford, in *The Man Who Shot Liberty Valance* (1962) found him fumbling rather familiarly as an indomitable good guy. The meanness, the cynicism, the murderous reality swirled around him. The film itself was good if undistinguished Ford, but it was a superior Western with the actor doing his professional duty as assigned. For all of Ford's expertise, the film, which had a screenplay by James Warner Bellah and Willis Goldbeck, was basically another reprise of the old cattlemen-versus-homesteaders theme. Furthermore, the picture also tacked on a verbose, drawn-out anticlimax.

The story of *The Man Who Shot Liberty Valance* is told in a long flashback by Stewart, now a famed state politician, who relates his early troubles in the lusty town of Shinbone. The town is mysteriously tolerant of Liberty Valance (Lee Marvin), a brutal, near-psychopath-

THE MAN WHO SHOT LIBERTY VALANCE (1962). With John Wayne

ic menace hired by cattle barons. Before Stewart finally shoots Valance—or did he?, and Ford waves this rather annoyingly as a whodunit teaser—and rises to national fame, he has been befriended by John Wayne (A Ford Stock Company favorite), as the local gun champion, and by smitten waitress Vera Miles.

Stewart did quite well in his role, as a kind of spunkier Destry, just as opposed to violence. Wayne, of course, was ideally suited to his comfortably meaty, standby role. Miss Miles, John Carradine, Jeanette Nolan, John Qualen, Andy Devine and Woody Strode lent helpful sideline assistance. However, Edmond O'Brien's babbling, drunken journalist and Marvin's bald villainy were a bit too much. The most impressive aspect, of the film perhaps, was its background, the town of Shinbone. The director had a field day evoking the lusty sights and sounds of the frontier community.

And now for Stewart came what virtually amounted to a minor role in a marvelous Ford Western, *Cheyenne Autumn* (1964). One might have expected, after their sterling collaboration in the smaller-scale *Two Rode Together*, and *Liberty Valance*, that Stewart would have played the male lead in this Western epic. But this role, that of a cavalry captain in charge of

steering a derelict Indian tribe to new quarters, was played extremely well by Richard Widmark.

Cheyenne Autumn, with a James R. Webb screenplay suggested by a Mari Sandoz book, was a passionate, moving and towering Western drama about a small band of Indians who in 1878 are shamefully removed from their ancient territory in the Yellowstone Southwest through official white trickery and who, although broken and starving, bravely attempt to return home, 1,500 miles distant.

In terms of character, fleshed out in a score of excellent performances, of dramatic sweep, magnificently authenticated in the surging pulse of the story and the richly panoramic settings, and of human pathos, with Ford carefully seeing to it that all components underscored the central tragedy, the film was a triumph for all concerned, with the old master director at the helm. With its tragic theme imprinted so vividly and affectingly on the traditional Western format of frontier conflict between the Indian and the white, Ford also extracted from this format some fierce, churning action, as in the scenes of the harsh skirmishes between the tribesmen and the cavalry. One sequence of the imprisonment of the Indians in a fort is heartrending. And the opening of the film, superbly tinted in the colors of dawn,

CHEYENNE AUTUMN (1964). As Wyatt Earp

CHEYENNE AUTUMN (1964). With Arthur Kennedy

is pure Ford, as a tribal delegation appears on the desert and stoically awaits government spokesmen who never appear, a bleak indication of the mistreatment and despair to come.

The acting of the huge cast did Ford proud. In addition to Widmark, as the conscience-stricken soldier, Carroll Baker and especially Karl Malden were effective in white roles, while Ricardo Montalban, Victor Jory, Gilbert Roland, Dolores Del Rio and Sal Mineo were fine as Cheyennes.

As Bosley Crowther indicated in his *New York Times* review of *Cheyenne Autumn,** "It is a stark and eye-opening symbolization of a shameful tendency that has prevailed in our national life—the tendency to be unjust and heartless to weaker peoples who get in the way of manifest destiny."

The *Times* critic, as did others, also indicated that a long comic sequence, where Stewart figures in the film, injected into *Cheyenne*

*December 24, 1964

118

Autumn at about midpoint, seemed at first anachronistic to the rest of the drama but eventually could be interpreted as Ford's put-down of traditional stereotyped attitudes in films toward the Indian as a curio. Stewart as Wyatt Earp was a mere component in this chapter, along with Arthur Kennedy as Doc Holliday and some other burly types who are abruptly shown roistering in a barroom in Dodge City, then whimsically deciding to ride out and watch the commotion firsthand,

only to scamper in fright from a lone Indian scout. The sequence itself was caustically amusing and Stewart and the others played it with leathery relish.

Stewart was little more than a footnote in *Cheyenne Autumn*, but in *The Rare Breed* (1966), co-starring with Maureen O'Hara, the actor was very much back in the Western saddle with accustomed star footage. It was the kind of easy, laconic Western comedy role he now had come to personify, when

THE RARE BREED (1966). With Maureen O'Hara

not sharpening his drawl flintily in drama such as *Two Rode Together*.

Written by Ric Hardman and directed by Andrew V. McLaglen, *The Rare Breed* exuded an easy, comfortable feeling best called entertainment. It amounted to a family-style serving of beef, amusingly salted at the edges and it had a neat idea to turn on, with the flame-haired Maureen as an English widow who has brought a prize Hereford bull to frontier Texas to revitalize longhorn breeding. She finds some ornery frontiersmen not the least bit interested—or amused.

McLaglen opens the film with a fine, hoof-thudding stampede, then levels off the rest on a steady, amusing level of nonviolence as the characterizations, all of them winningly played, take over. Miss O'Hara was delightful as the spunky, pretty newcomer to the American rangeland, tart-spoken but properly genteel as the hostile men began to accept her cattle-breeding campaign and appreciate her personally. Britain's Juliet Mills scored nicely as her daughter in her Hollywood debut, and David Brian and young Don Galloway were also good.

But *The Rare Breed* was stolen lock, stock and barrel by Brian Keith, whose infatuation with Miss O'Hara transforms him overnight from a shaggy, thunderous Scotsman to a pliable, lovelorn lamb.

Keith, soon to begin a successful television series of his own, did notably well by this role, one of his juiciest up to this time, making it both funny and touching.

Even so, Stewart's wise, quiet assurance radiated like a Franklin stove from the center of the film and toward the end, when the plot veered toward outright sentimentality, he steadied it with unstrained simplicity. Here was a role he undoubtedly enjoyed doing; this was a likeable movie.

Firecreek (1968) was hardly likable, but it was infinitely better. Furthermore, this modest and occasionally powerful Western, from Warner-Seven Arts, reunited Stewart and his old friend, Henry Fonda, for the first time in twenty years (*A Miracle Can Happen*). Both of them were superb as two frontier guys, good and bad.

The film, moreover, unfolded in a tiny, dusty Western town and looked as though it had been made for a dime, something that pictorially tightened it like a hangman's knot, with the characters and action kept in clear, close rein by Vincent McEveety, a fine new director from television. In the screenplay by Calvin Clements, Stewart was a peaceful farmer and part-time sheriff aroused to wrath after five killers, led by Fonda, have arrived and proceeded to terrorize the small, quaking village. Finally

120

FIRECREEK (1968). With Henry Fonda

BANDOLERO! (1968). With Dean Martin

goaded into action, Stewart simmers and explodes. In a way, *Firecreek* was a kind of small-scale *High Noon*.

The beauty of the movie was the professional, simple treatment, the performances and the terse, often razor-sharp dialogue that either rounded out a characterization or propelled the action forward. The sideline casting of the villagers drew good work from Inger Stevens, J.

Robert Porter, Dean Jagger, Ed Begley, Jay C. Flippen and others. McEveety starts the picture at a casual pace, with Fonda partially disabled and his pals deliberately causing mischief that leads to murder, a hanging and that final gun showdown between the two stars, with Stewart compelled to act on behalf of the cowed, mistreated villagers.

Stewart and Fonda are amazingly

effective in this economical little Western, both separately and together. In the scenes where McEveety starts building a chilling crescendo, as the pair of enemies-on-sight begin to feel out each other's strengths and weaknesses, there is such scorching realistic intimacy, tempered with a suggestion of amused irony on the part of both actors, that a viewer might have wondered what the two men, friends since the early thirties, were really thinking face to face.

Their performances are like flint on steel, culminating in that volcanic showdown when Stewart, wounded and hobbling, almost goes berserk with righteous rage as he and Fonda stalk each other. (The actors were to make still another picture together two years later, a sporting but rather obvious package of prairie salt titled *The Cheyenne Social Club*.)

Dean Martin was no Fonda as a co-star for Stewart in *Bandolero!* (1968), a rather lackluster attempt at an adult Western set in post-Civil War Texas, with standard gun-blasting and appropriately earthy phrases spiking rather murky motivational palaver on all sides. In this Fox release, Andrew V. McLaglen's direction and James Lee Barrett's screenplay were hard put to keep things interesting, even convincing, with Stewart, as Martin's older, wiser brother and the latter brashly leading a criminal gang and eventually kidnaping Raquel Welch, as the luscious widow of one of their victims. Naturally she falls for Martin. George Kennedy played a chase-leading sheriff, a thankless role requiring little more than energy. Stewart at least seemed relaxed and professional, which put him several notches ahead of the others.

The reunion two years later of Stewart and Fonda in *The Cheyenne Social Club* (1970) was gamely accepted by most viewers as a friendly, ribald-edged throwback, a leathery salute, to the good old days. There was familiarity, undoubtedly, in the sight of the two grizzled, aging cowpokes shuffling around with harmless grins only to spring into action in a saloon fight and a shoot-up with some mean hombres after one of them brutally pummels the ever-sugary Shirley Jones, a lady in spite of the bawdy house she runs.

That was "The Cheyenne Social Club," the main gimmick and the one joke of the movie, under Gene Kelly's limber direction, and with a tangy script by James Lee Barrett—the sight of the stars, two sheepish old boys, gravitating toward Miss Jones' house and more or less becoming mascots of the pretty inmates, who behaved like Louisa May Alcott's *Little Women*.

THE CHEYENNE SOCIAL CLUB (1970). With Henry Fonda

FOOLS' PARADE (1971). With Strother Martin and George Kennedy

As the film jogged along archly, the picture never missed a blue chance to suggest more going on than met the eye in the parlor and corridors.

Fools' Parade (1971), Stewart's seventy-third movie and his last one to date, was a strangely satisfying time-killer of a film, obviously not meant to be taken too seriously.

The plot of James Lee Barrett's script, based on the novel by Davis Grubb, was different, to say the least. The one catch to the film, capably directed by Andrew V. McLaglen, was a contrived windup.

Stewart played one of three convicts released from a West Virginia prison in the mid-thirties and trying in vain to collect the sum of $25,000, owed him after his forty years of imprisonment by a crafty, reluctant bank. What followed was intriguing and entertaining, with a well-rendered, restrained feeling for the background of the times and a sharply detailed atmosphere of suspense as the aging, new civilian and his helpful colleagues doggedly plot to get Stewart's hefty remittance.

Stewart was excellent as the cagey, hard-headed protagonist and the others were very good indeed, including Kurt Russell and Strother Martin as his confederates, Kathy Cannon as a girl smitten with Russell, and George Kennedy as a pious fly in the ointment. One critic declared that Stewart looked like a taller William Faulkner, with his white hair and mustache, and even thought that the character he portrayed seemed Faulknerian (with a removable glass eye). The resemblance was irrelevant, for after seventy-three movies, James Stewart was not about to skip gracefully into the role of one of the film colony's retired elder statesmen, whatever he looked like in *Fools' Parade*.

On July 2, 1970, it was announced that James Stewart would join the long list of Hollywood stars who had made weekly television series. The sixty-two-year-old actor was expected to sign a contract with the National Broadcasting Company to star in a weekly half-hour series for the 1971-72 season. Hal Kanter was to produce the program for Warner Bros. Television. The star had recently concluded his highly successful appearance on Broadway in the revival of *Harvey*.

The less said about *The Jimmy Stewart Show*, which lasted one season, the better. As a family comedy, it was a perfectly respectable series, better than some downright moronic counterparts, but far below the rounded appeal of a long-running series like *Father Knows Best*, the Robert Young-Jane Wyatt perennial. In this show, appearing as a stereotyped image of himself, complete with slight stammer, shy, mumbling charm and a familiar, homespun coating, Stewart played a college professor getting into "cute" situations with his family. At least there was no exasperating sound track of laughter but the series, which did have a certain warm integrity, proceeded to wax heavier and heavier, succumbing to banality.

Stewart was successful the second time; *Hawkins* hit the bull's-eye. The ninety-minute series on the Columbia Broadcasting System, rotating on Tuesday with *Shaft* and a movie series, was "created" and is produced by David Karp; the executive producer is Norman Felton. This is the Jimmy Stewart show that should have occurred in the first place, although many Stewart fans may still wonder why the veteran saddle-rider didn't join the bronco parade on the home screen. Furthermore, this crime-detection series arrived in October 1973, in a season glutted with new programs and reruns having to do with detectives and police. Yet it stood out, as did Stewart, as one of the season's best.

The pilot feature, shown a bit earlier as a "special" program before the regular series began, was impressively intelligent suspense, carefully draped to fit Stewart's lanky form and personality. As Hawkins, a nationally famous criminal attorney from West Virginia, with a folksy manner and a placid core of hard common sense, he was summoned to California for a double-slaying case in a wealthy home. At the side of Billy Jim Hawkins, as a kind of rustic Doctor Watson, was his cousin, R.J., played by Strother Martin (one of Stewart's convict pals from *Fools' Parade*).

With Dennis Larson on "The Jimmy Stewart Show"

This spearhead segment, aptly titled *Hawkins on Murder*, was gripping, with Stewart digging steadily into the case until he told R.J. during a courtroom recess, "And now I'm gonna pull one of the dirtiest tricks I've ever done." Whereupon, he mercilessly grills, on the witness stand, his own defendant, a neurotic young girl already on the verge of insanity, a workout that forces the real culprit (an aunt) to come forward and confess out of protective love.

But it was the later, official opening segment of *Hawkins*, presented over the CBS network in October, 1973, that jolted the critics, because of its sexual candor, and also had most of them reaching for top-praise adjectives. A bit startled to find good old Jimmy Stewart in a strin-

As detective Hawkins, in Hawkins on Murder, March, 1973

In an episode of the "Hawkins" series, with Cameron Mitchell and William Smithers

gently frank drama involving Hollywood's homosexual community, they also hailed the program as first-rate, adult entertainment that sharply integrated and did not exploit questionable material.

On the strength of this segment, *The New York Times* called the program "the most impressively acted, written, directed and photographed of the new series so far this season."*

Sheree North and Cameron

*October 2, 1973, reviewed by John O'Connor.

Mitchell also gave noteworthy performances in the episode, titled "Murder In Movieland," with Stewart scenting out the facts behind the killing, during an adulterous tryst, of a bisexual hustler who has attracted an alcoholic, ex-movie star, played by Miss North. Mitchell was her understanding husband. Jud Taylor directed this opening segment of *Hawkins*.

The same quality of reality, blending a puzzling whodunit angle, expert playing and an admirable treatment, prevailed in subsequent episodes involving the murder of a sports impresario and the dispatch of an innuendo-purring newscaster.

Times—and the Hollywood studios that brought James Stewart fame and fortune—have changed. *Hawkins*, which hops around the film capital considerably for location scenes, is based with other popular series in a converted segment of MGM's formidable old Stage 15. The huge shed was once the largest enclosure on the lot back in the golden days, housing palaces and Esther Williams-style pools, even the enormous frozen rink built for *Ice Follies of 1939*, one of the actor's earliest and worst entrapments.

Down the street on Lot 2, where other perennial sets have given way to television-production construction, there sits a pleasant two-story frame house, once the movie residence of Stewart's and June Allyson's Mr. and Mrs. Monty Stratton; the house was recently utilized for *Hawkins*. At last report, the famous, swanky old house used for *The Philadelphia Story* and many subsequent movies has survived the bulldozers.

STEWART: THE MAN AND THE ACTOR

Casting a reminiscent eye around the lot during a recent break during *Hawkins*, Stewart did not bite the hand that launched him. He cited the skill of the MGM craftsmen, the magic builders who overnight could whip up a desert, an iceberg, a battlefield or a lunar landscape. According to the actor, there was a good feeling of security in being part of the MGM "family."

"Don't believe those clichés," he said, about MGM being a factory. "The executives were not power-drunk tyrants. Producers and directors and writers had freedom and were treated very well. And actors were treated so well. You worked all the time, fifty-two weeks a year. They protected you . . . and took care of your publicity."*

Stewart's positive, even appreciative attitude toward the high-powered operation of what was once the world's largest motion-picture studio is not exactly widespread. The only other major MGM graduate more or less echoing the same feeling was, somewhat surprisingly, Lana Turner. "I had no complaints," the actress told this writer, looking puzzled at my question, during a promotion tour for her 1966 film, *Madame X*. June Allyson once told me in her Hollywood living room, eyes widening

TV Guide, March 2, 1974, interviewed by Maurice Zolotow.

for stress, that "MGM is *not* an easy studio to work for." And Elizabeth Taylor succinctly declared during my post-*Cleopatra* interview for *The New York Times* that "to the studio all those years I was nothing but a business commodity, just like a piece of steel."

In truth, James Maitland Stewart at sixty-six would seem to have little cause not to appreciate his first Hollywood alma mater. From savings, investments and salary over a span of thirty-nine years (with his wartime service interval), the actor is generally considered to be one of the wealthiest men in Hollywood. Stewart and his wife live comfortably in Beverly Hills, move quietly and easily in the top establishment society of the film capital and show no inclination to hitch up to the international flash of the gossip-column favorites, the jet set.

The actor is in a position to do exactly as he pleases. For instance, during the *Hawkins* filmings, he chooses to carry to work a battered antique lunch pail and to eat lunch in his trailer dressing room, studying his lines. Two years ago, in the Alumni Day parade at Princeton, Stewart looked like any number of other pleasant, aging graduates

132

MR. SMITH GOES TO WASHINGTON (1939). Jeff Smith at point of collapse

gamely traipsing down Nassau Street in the wake of the school mascot, Mike the Tiger. Being a world-famous man, Stewart's tall, lanky frame and familiar face were closely scrutinized during the parade and other events of his forty-fifth class reunion.

The actor joined Joshua Logan, his old schoolmate and now a noted Broadway director, for an official, local interview about the school's Triangle Club, the nation's oldest college musical touring company. "Triangle put me in direct contact with the theater," Stewart remembered.* As an undergraduate in the winter of 1931, the architecture major won warm praise for playing the lead in Triangle's merry production called *Spanish Blades*; an old photo shows a young, costumed Stewart, debonair and smiling, with a natty, sleek moustache and cape. After two Triangle shows, he said, "there was no doubt in my mind that I wanted to go into acting."

In an earlier interview,** asked if he thought the movies of yore were superior to the ones now, Stewart said he believed today's output, while better technically, had a sameness to them. "There are just too many pictures based on violence and sex." (He has yet to make a genuine sample of either species; the closest real brush with sex was the harmless presence, as a symbolic gag, of the tempestuous Mlle. Bardot in that comedy misfire, *Dear Brigitte*.) Stewart continued: "If it were true that the sex-violence kind of thing is what people will pay money to see, then why is the Disney outfit in better shape than any other studio in town? What I'd really like to see now in pictures is simply more variety."

Harking back to his Princeton teeth-cutting on a stage, Stewart said he didn't think that television provided the best training for the young. "And there aren't as many jobs in it as you might think," he added. "I've always felt that the best way to learn to act was simply to act. TV just doesn't give the experience and varied roles a youngster needs to learn his craft."

Stewart has often spoken longingly of the bygone, golden days of Broadway when he began, as a time of hard work, varied opportunities in many productions, and also as a time of joy, despite the grimness of the Depression.

The blackest moment in the actor's personal life occurred in June 1969, during the filming of *The Cheyenne Social Club*, when Stewart and his wife received the news of the death of their son,

The New York Times, May 7, 1972, interviewed by Bill Kovacic.
**New York Sunday News*, June 21, 1970, interviewed by Bob Lardine.

THE NAKED SPUR (1953).
As Howard Kemp

Ronald, by Mrs. Stewart's previous marriage, who was killed in action in Vietnam at the age of twenty-four. Commenting on their loss the following year, the actor said, "Neither my wife nor I have any bitterness. We've gotten hundreds and hundreds of letters." He added: "I believe in the cause he died for."*

As a man who had spent twenty-seven years in the military, Stewart also staunchly defended the American military image, whose "principles and standards I learned made me a better civilian."

As a staunch Republican, the actor is an ardent Nixon supporter (or was until the Watergate scandal), who not only participated in the campaign for the President's reelection but narrated a nine-minute campaign documentary movie about Mrs. Nixon. Stewart is a close friend of John Wayne, a well-known Republican and arch-conservative, and with another of his close friends, Fred MacMurray, Stewart has been a golfing companion of Mr. Nixon. As a member of the board of directors of the Boy Scouts of America and a trustee at Princeton for four years back in the early 1960s, Stewart was a keen youth-watcher as campus unrest exploded across the country several years ago. Asked if his own

youngsters were involved, back in 1970, Stewart said placidly:

"I can tell you for certain that they're not breaking any windows. Kelly is a freshman at Stanford. Her twin, Judy, attends Lewis and Clark. Both are doing their work. Michael just finished graduate school at Claremont College with a degree in education. He didn't throw any rocks while he was there." Stewart, like Wayne, attributed much of the dissension and unrest to Communism. "I don't think there's any question that the Communists are behind a great deal of unrest in this country. In addition, I feel they are still a potential danger to show business."**

However, Stewart does see certain similarities between some of his youthful performances on the screen and the currently popular antiheroes. For instance, he considers *Mr. Smith Goes to Washington*, back in 1939, to be antiestablishment in its questioning of big government and its cynical view of the lack of integrity in high places. But most of the new movies don't impress him. He disagrees with new actors and directors who rejoice over a chance for complete realism as a reflection of the human condition. "That's okay," says Stewart, "but it's not all a movie should do."

*The New York Times, February 22, 1970, interviewed by Judy Klemesrud.

**New York Sunday News, June 21, 1970, interviewed by Bob Lardine.

REAR WINDOW (1954). Jeff registers fear.

Stewart has quietly said in recent years that he always secretly felt that his Oscar for *The Philadelphia Story* in 1940 came a year late. "But I was up against too much competition." Perhaps, he conceded, there was Academy sentimentality involved in his copping the award the following year, but that was all right. "The Academy get-together enables your fellow workers to give you a pat on the back." Since the Oscar ceremony has become a major television attraction, commanding a huge international audience of home watchers, Stewart finds it "kind of cold and a little dull."

But there was nothing cold or dull about the tall, thin, slightly stooped and graying actor who mounted the stage on Oscar night in 1961, shortly before the death of Gary Cooper, and thrust an honorary statuette at the camera, his voice breaking and with tears in his eyes. "Coop," said Stewart hoarsely, and all of Hollywood knew he was addressing a dying legend who was watching the ceremony from his bed at home, "this is for you from all of us. We're all very proud of you, Coop, all of us are terribly proud."

The image of James Stewart as an actor is a composite portrait of a worker at his craft, improving methodically and leisurely over a period of many years before the camera. Technically, he has worked at it continually, by his account, even, for instance, during the making of such a 1963 trifle as *Take Her, She's Mine*.

"That slow drawl," he said during a break, "has become too slow. I seem to be padding my lines, and it's not a good thing. I like to think that now my style should be more precise. Not as much hemming and hawing as before." He said he had taken inventory after watching *You Can't Take It With You*, *Mr. Smith Goes to Washington* and *The Philadelphia Story* and others at home on television.

"My reactions to a situation have never been particularly subtle," he continued. "Not too broad, either. I think I've developed in my ability to listen to the other actors in a scene. There is too much acting in which one actor uses another mainly to cue him."*

The Stewart eyes have a watchful air now, with a fixed, piercing candor, as subtle pauses and even subtler shifts of expression all merge authoritatively and with seeming, deceptive simplicity of expression on the creased, aging countenance of an American screen legend. Although the Stewart image is now indelible, it developed with persistent professionalism over many

The New York Times, May 30, 1963, interviewed by Murray Schumach.

THE SPIRIT OF ST. LOUIS (1957). Lindbergh prepares for take-off.

years, from the staunch, young apple-pie idealist of the prewar years, through the postwar Westerns that signaled his maturity and the outstanding ones that crystallized it, spiced with the color and tingle of the Hitchcock plumcakes. In a way, it was inevitable that *Anatomy of a Murder* should eventually trigger a Hawkins, piping the American legend into the American home.

What does not change in Stewart's performances is the unmistakable trademark of that drawl, as widely imitated by impressionists as the voices of Cary Grant, James Cagney and Edward G. Robinson. Catch a showing of that charming old Eddy-MacDonald antique, *Rose Marie* (Stewart's second movie) and listen to the youthful actor as he spots Miss MacDonald's approaching horse, grabs a rifle and rushes to the window of the remote cabin in the Canadian wilderness.

"Sis," he greets her anxiously with a tense, boyish crack in his voice, "what're you doing here?"

"As an actor," Stewart has maintained, "you have to develop a style that suits you and pursue it, not just develop a bag of tricks. The stage teaches you all sorts of basic things. But the movies is a different ball game. On Broadway, you have to sustain a mood for twenty minutes—in movies, for twenty seconds. Back in my early Broad-

way days, you didn't act by religion or method. There was no cult. You were just told to learn your craft and you did."*

On the set, Stewart's personal habits have changed little over the years. Eating lunch alone, Stewart usually concentrates on his script, often planning ahead for the next day. "It's much more difficult to maintain a consistent performance in a movie than in a play," he has said. He also calls the theater "a tougher racket."

Unlike many major stars, Stewart can't see himself as a director, even with his wide experience in theater and films. "It takes a lot of understanding of all forms of the art, and I haven't got it." Of his two favorite directors, he said, "John Ford knows how to tell a story and uses a minimum of dialogue because he believes movies are basically visual. Hitchcock's the same way. But I'm no Ford or Hitchcock.**

Nor has Stewart any thoughts of pulling out of the profession, especially with *Hawkins* a success and with a distinguished film career to which he can return comfortably almost any time he pleases:

"I don't want to retire. The audience will tell me when it's time to

---

*Quoted in 1970 by columnist Joyce Haber.
**Cue* magazine, April 21, 1962, interviewed by Jesse Zunser.

As star of television program, "The American West of John Ford" (1971)

quit. I love making movies. I've never felt it was a boring job. It's not only fun, but it's rewarding and exciting to me. I feel that I'm accomplishing something, as when someone comes up to me and says, 'I don't know if it means anything to you but you have given me and my family a great deal of enjoyment over the years.' "*

*New York Sunday News, June 21, 1970.

BIBLIOGRAPHY

Griffith, Richard. *Anatomy of a Motion Picture*. St. Martin's Press, New York, 1959.

Martin, Pete. "Shyest Guy in Hollywood." *Saturday Evening Post*, September 15, 1951.

McClure, Arthur F., Jones, Ken D., and Twomey, Alfred E. *The Films of James Stewart*. A.S. Barnes and Company, South Brunswick and New York, 1970.

The New York Times Film Reviews, Volumes 2-6 (1932-1970). The New York Times and Arno Press, New York, 1970.

Parish, James Robert and Bowers, Ronald L. *The MGM Stock Company*. Arlington House, New Rochelle, N.Y., 1973

Truffaut, François. *Hitchcock*. Simon & Schuster, New York, 1967.

Zolotow, Maurice, "Waal, In the Old Days, Ya See . . .", *TV Guide* March 2, 1974.

THE FILMS OF JAMES STEWART

The director's name follows the release date. A (c) following the release date indicates that the film was in color. Sp indicates Screenplay and b/o indicates based/on.

1. THE MURDER MAN. MGM, 1935. *Tim Whelan*. Sp: Whelan and John C. Higgins, b/o story by Whelan and Guy Bolton. Cast: Spencer Tracy, Virginia Bruce, Lionel Atwill, Harvey Stephens.

2. ROSE MARIE. MGM, 1936. *W.S. Van Dyke*. Sp: Frances Goodrich, Albert Hackett, and Alice Duer Miller, b/o operetta by Otto Harbach and Oscar Hammerstein 2d. Cast: Jeanette MacDonald, Nelson Eddy, Reginald Owen, George Regas, Allan Jones, David Niven. Previously filmed in 1928 and remade in 1954.

3. NEXT TIME WE LOVE. Universal, 1936. *Edward H. Griffith*. Sp: Melville Baker, b/o novel *Next Time We Live* by Ursula Parrott. Cast: Margaret Sullavan, Ray Milland, Grant Mitchell, Anna Demetrio.

4. WIFE VS. SECRETARY. MGM, 1936. *Clarence Brown*. Sp: Norman Krasna, Alice Duer Miller and John Lee Mahin, b/o story by Faith Baldwin. Cast: Clark Gable, Jean Harlow, Myrna Loy, May Robson, George Barbier.

5. SMALL TOWN GIRL. MGM, 1936. *William A. Wellman*. Sp: John Lee Mahin and Edith Fitzgerald, b/o novel by Ben Ames Williams. Cast: Janet Gaynor, Robert Taylor, Binnie Barnes, Lewis Stone, Frank Craven.

6. SPEED. MGM, 1936. *Edwin L. Marin*. Sp: Michael Fessier, b/o story by Milton Krims and Larry Bachman. Cast: Wendy Barrie, Una Merkel, Weldon Heyburn, Ted Healy.

7. THE GORGEOUS HUSSY. MGM, 1936. *Clarence Brown*. Sp: Ainsworth Morgan and Stephen Morehouse Avery, b/o novel by Samuel Hopkins Adams. Cast: Joan Crawford, Robert Taylor, Lionel Barrymore, Franchot Tone, Melvyn Douglas, Beulah Bondi.

8. BORN TO DANCE. MGM, 1936. *Roy Del Ruth*. Sp: Sid Silvers and Jack McGowan, b/o story by McGowan, Silvers and B.G. De Sylva. Cast: Eleanor Powell, Virginia Bruce, Una Merkel, Sid Silvers, Frances Langford, Alan Dinehart, Buddy Ebsen.

9. AFTER THE THIN MAN. MGM, 1936. *W.S. Van Dyke*. Sp: Frances Goodrich and Albert Hackett, b/o story by Dashiell Hammett. Cast: William Powell, Myrna Loy, Elissa Landi, Joseph Calleia, Jessie Ralph, Sam Levene.

10. SEVENTH HEAVEN. 20th Century-Fox, 1937. *Henry King*. Sp: Melville Baker, b/o play by Austin Strong. Cast: Simone Simon, Jean Hersholt, Gale Sondergaard, Gregory Ratoff. Previously filmed in 1927.

11. THE LAST GANGSTER. MGM, 1937. *Edward Ludwig*. Sp: John Lee Mahin, b/o story by William A. Wellman and Robert Carson. Cast: Edward G. Robinson, Rose Stradner, Lionel Stander, John Carradine, Sidney Blackmer.

12. NAVY BLUE AND GOLD. MGM, 1937. *Sam Wood*. Sp: George Bruce, b/o his novel. Cast: Robert Young, Lionel Barrymore, Florence Rice, Billie Burke, Tom Brown.

13. OF HUMAN HEARTS. MGM, 1938. *Clarence Brown*. Sp: Bradbury Foote, b/o Honore Morrow's story *Benefits Forgot*. Cast: Walter Huston, Beulah Bondi, Gene Reynolds, Guy Kibbee, Charles Coburn, John Carradine, Ann Rutherford.

14. VIVACIOUS LADY. RKO Radio, 1938. *George Stevens*. Sp: P.J. Wolfson and Ernest Pagano, b/o story by I.A.R. Wylie. Cast: Ginger Rogers, James Ellison, Beulah Bondi, Charles Coburn, Frances Mercer, Jack Carson.

15. THE SHOPWORN ANGEL. MGM, 1938. *H.C. Potter*. Sp: Waldo Salt, b/o Dana Burnet's story *Private Pettigrew's Girl*. Cast: Margaret Sullavan, Walter Pidgeon, Hattie McDaniel, Nat Pendleton, Alan Curtis. Previously filmed in 1928.

16. YOU CAN'T TAKE IT WITH YOU. Columbia, 1938. *Frank Capra*. Sp: Robert Riskin b/o play by George S. Kaufman and Moss Hart. Cast: Jean Arthur, Lionel Barrymore, Edward Arnold, Mischa Auer, Ann Miller, Spring Byington, Samuel S. Hinds, Donald Meek, H.B. Warner, Halliwell Hobbes.

17. MADE FOR EACH OTHER. A Selznick International Picture, released by United Artists, 1939. *John Cromwell*. Sp: Jo Swerling. Cast: Carole Lombard, Charles Coburn, Lucile Watson, Eddie Quillan, Alma Kruger.

18. ICE FOLLIES OF 1939. MGM,1939. *Reinhold Schunzel*. Sp: Leonard Praskins. Cast: Joan Crawford, Lew Ayres, Lewis Stone, Bess Ehrhardt, Lionel Stander. Sequence in color.

19. IT'S A WONDERFUL WORLD. MGM, 1939. *W.S. Van Dyke*. Sp: Ben Hecht, b/o story by Hecht and Herman J. Mankiewicz. Cast: Claudette Colbert, Guy Kibbee, Nat Pendleton, Frances Drake, Edgar Kennedy.

20. MR. SMITH GOES TO WASHINGTON. Columbia, 1939. *Frank Capra*. Sp: Sidney Buchman, b/o story by Lewis R. Foster. Cast: Jean Arthur, Claude Rains, Edward Arnold, Thomas Mitchell, Guy Kibbee, Beulah Bondi, Harry Carey.

21. DESTRY RIDES AGAIN. Universal, 1939. *George Marshall*. Sp: Felix Jackson, Gertrude Purcell, and Henry Myers, b/o novel by Max Brand. Cast: Marlene Dietrich, Charles Winninger, Mischa Auer, Brian Donlevy, Irene Hervey, Una Merkel. Previously filmed in 1932 and remade in 1954 as *Destry*.

22. THE SHOP AROUND THE CORNER. MGM, 1940. *Ernst Lubitsch*. Sp: Samson Raphaelson, b/o play by Nikolaus Laszlo. Cast: Margaret Sullavan, Frank Morgan, Joseph Schildkraut, Sara Haden, Felix Bressart, William Tracy. Remade in 1949 as *In the Good Old Summertime*.

23. THE MORTAL STORM. MGM, 1940. *Frank Borzage*. Sp: Claudine West, Andersen Ellis, and George Froeschel, b/o novel by Phyllis Bottome. Cast: Margaret Sullavan, Robert Young, Frank Morgan, Robert Stack, Bonita Granville, Irene Rich, Gene Reynolds, Maria Ouspenskaya.

24. NO TIME FOR COMEDY. Warner Bros., 1940. *William Keighley*. Sp: Julius J. and Philip G. Epstein, b/o play by S.N. Behrman. Cast: Rosalind Russell, Charles Ruggles, Genevieve Tobin, Allyn Joslyn, Louise Beavers.

25. THE PHILADELPHIA STORY. MGM, 1940. *George Cukor*. Sp: Donald Ogden Stewart, b/o play by Philip Barry. Cast: Cary Grant, Katharine Hepburn, Ruth Hussey, John Howard, Roland Young, John Halliday, Mary Nash, Virginia Weidler. Remade in 1956 as *High Society*.

26. COME LIVE WITH ME. MGM, 1941. *Clarence Brown*. Sp: Patterson McNutt, b/o story by Virginia Van Upp. Cast: Hedy Lamarr, Ian Hunter, Verree Teasdale, Donald Meek, Barton MacLane.

27. POT O'GOLD. United Artists, 1941. *George Marshall*. Sp: Walter De Leon, b/o story by Andrew Bennison, Monte Brice, and Harry Tugend. Cast: Paulette Goddard, Horace Heidt, Charles Winninger, Mary Gordon.

28. ZIEGFELD GIRL. MGM, 1941. *Robert Z. Leonard*. Sp: Marguerite Roberts and Sonya Levien, b/o story by William Anthony McGuire. Cast: Judy Garland, Hedy Lamarr, Lana Turner, Tony Martin, Ian Hunter, Philip Dorn, Dan Dailey, Jackie Cooper.

29. IT'S A WONDERFUL LIFE. A Liberty Film, released by RKO Radio, 1946. *Frank Capra*. Sp: Frances Goodrich, Albert Hackett and Capra. Cast: Donna Reed, Lionel Barrymore, Thomas Mitchell, Beulah Bondi, Henry Travers, Ward Bond.

30. MAGIC TOWN. RKO, 1947. *William A. Wellman*. Sp: Robert Riskin, b/o story by Riskin and Joseph Krumgold. Cast: Jane Wyman, Kent Smith, Ned Sparks, Wallace Ford, Ann Doran, Regis Toomey.

31. CALL NORTHSIDE 777. 20th Century-Fox, 1948. *Henry Hathaway*. Sp: James Cady and Jay Dratler, adapted by Leonard Hoffman and Quentin Reynolds, b/o article by James P. McGuire. Cast: Richard Conte, Lee J. Cobb, Helen Walker, Betty Garde, Howard Smith.

32. A MIRACLE CAN HAPPEN (later retitled: ON OUR MERRY WAY). United Artists, 1948. *King Vidor* and *Leslie Fenton*. Sp: Laurence Stallings and Lou Breslow, b/o story by Arch Oboler. Cast: Burgess Meredith, Paulette Goddard, Henry Fonda, Dorothy Ford, Eduardo Ciannelli, Dorothy Lamour.

33. ROPE. Warner Bros., 1948. (c) *Alfred Hitchcock*. Sp: Arthur Laurents, adapted by Hume Cronyn from play *Rope's End* by Patrick Hamilton. Cast: John Dall, Farley Granger, Sir Cedric Hardwicke, Constance Collier, Douglas Dick, Joan Chandler.

34. YOU GOTTA STAY HAPPY. Universal-International, 1948. *H.C. Potter*. Sp: Karl Tunberg, b/o story by Robert Carson. Cast: Joan Fontaine, Eddie Albert, Roland Young, Willard Parker, Percy Kilbride.

35. THE STRATTON STORY. MGM, 1949. *Sam Wood*. Sp: Douglas Morrow and Guy Trosper, b/o story by Morrow. Cast: June Allyson, Frank Morgan, Agnes Moorehead, Bill Williams, Bruce Cowling.

36. MALAYA. MGM, 1950. *Richard Thorpe*. Sp: Frank Fenton, b/o story by Manchester Boddy. Cast: Spencer Tracy, Valentina Cortese, Sydney Greenstreet, John Hodiak, Lionel Barrymore.

37. WINCHESTER .73. Universal-International, 1950. *Anthony Mann*. Sp: Robert L. Richards and Borden Chase, b/o story by Stuart N. Lake. Cast: Shelley Winters, Dan Duryea, Stephen McNally, Millard Mitchell, Will Geer.

38. BROKEN ARROW. 20th Century-Fox, 1950. (c) *Delmer Daves*. Sp: Michael Blankfort, b/o novel *Blood Brother*, by Elliott Arnold. Cast: Jeff Chandler, Debra Paget, Basil Ruysdael, Will Geer, Arthur Hunnicutt.

39. THE JACKPOT. 20th Century-Fox, 1950. *Walter Lang*. Sp: Phoebe and Henry Ephron, b/o article by John McNulty. Cast: Barbara Hale, James Gleason, Fred Clark, Alan Mowbray, Patricia Medina, Natalie Wood.

40. HARVEY. Universal-International, 1950. *Henry Koster*. Sp: Mary C. Chase and Oscar Brodney, b/o play by Mrs. Chase. Cast: Josephine Hull, Peggy Dow, Charles Drake, Cecil Kellaway, Victoria Horne, Jesse White.

41. NO HIGHWAY IN THE SKY. 20th Century-Fox, 1951. *Henry Koster*. Sp: R.C.Sherriff, Oscar Millard, and Alec Coppell, b/o novel by Nevil Shute. Cast: Marlene Dietrich, Glynis Johns, Jack Hawkins, Janette Scott, Elizabeth Allan, Ronald Squire.

42. THE GREATEST SHOW ON EARTH. Paramount, 1952. (c) *Cecil B. DeMille*. Sp: Fredric M. Frank, Barré Lyndon and Theodore St. John, b/o story by Frank Cavett, Frank and St. John. Cast: Betty Hutton, Cornel Wilde, Charlton Heston, Lyle Bettger, Gloria Grahame, Dorothy Lamour, Lawrence Tierney.

43. BEND OF THE RIVER. Universal-International, 1952. (c) *Anthony Mann*. Sp: Borden Chase, b/o novel by Bill Gulick. Cast: Arthur Kennedy, Julia Adams, Rock Hudson, Jay C. Flippen, Lori Nelson.

44. CARBINE WILLIAMS. MGM, 1952. *Richard Thorpe*. Sp: Art Cohn. Cast: Jean Hagen, Wendell Corey, Carl Benton Reid, Otto Hulett, Rhys Williams.

45. THE NAKED SPUR. MGM, 1953. (c). *Anthony Mann*. Sp: Sam Rolfe and Harold Jack Bloom. Cast: Janet Leigh, Robert Ryan, Ralph Meeker, Millard Mitchell.

46. THUNDER BAY. Universal-International, 1953. (c) *Anthony Mann*. Sp: Gil Doud and John Michael Hayes, b/o story by Hayes. Cast: Joanne Dru, Gilbert Roland, Dan Duryea, Marcia Henderson, Jay C. Flippen.

47. THE GLENN MILLER STORY. Universal-International, 1954. (c) *Anthony Mann*. Sp: Valentine Davies and Oscar Brodney. Cast: June Allyson, Charles Drake, George Tobias, Henry Morgan, Marion Ross.

48. REAR WINDOW. Paramount, 1954. (c) *Alfred Hitchcock*. Sp: John Michael Hayes, b/o short story by Cornell Woolrich. Cast: Grace Kelly, Wendell Corey, Thelma Ritter, Raymond Burr, Judith Evelyn, Ross Bagdasarian, Georgine Darcy.

49. THE FAR COUNTRY. Universal-International, 1955. (c) *Anthony Mann*. Sp: Borden Chase. Cast: Ruth Roman, Corinne Calvet, Walter Brennan, John McIntire, Jay C. Flippen.

50. STRATEGIC AIR COMMAND. Paramount, 1955. (c) *Anthony Mann*. Sp: Valentine Davies and Beirne Lay, Jr., b/o story by Lay. Cast: June Allyson, Frank Lovejoy, Barry Sullivan, Alex Nicol, Bruce Bennett.

51. THE MAN FROM LARAMIE. Columbia, 1955 (c) *Anthony Mann*. Sp: Philip Yordan and Frank Burt, b/o story by Thomas Flynn. Cast: Arthur Kennedy, Donald Crisp, Cathy O'Donnell, Alex Nicol, Aline MacMahon, Wallace Ford.

52. THE MAN WHO KNEW TOO MUCH. Paramount, 1956. (c) *Alfred Hitchcock*. Sp: John Michael Hayes, b/o story by Charles Bennett and D.B. Wyndham-Lewis. Cast: Doris Day, Brenda de Banzie, Bernard Miles, Ralph Truman, Christopher Olsen, Daniel Gelin. Previously filmed in 1934.

53. THE SPIRIT OF ST. LOUIS. Warner Bros., 1957. (c) *Billy Wilder*. Sp: Wilder and Wendell Mayes, adapted by Charles Lederer, b/o book by Charles A. Lindbergh. Cast: Murray Hamilton, Patricia Smith, Marc Connelly, Bartlett Robinson, Arthur Space.

54. NIGHT PASSAGE. Universal, 1957. (c) *James Neilson*. Sp: Borden Chase, b/o story by Norman Fox. Cast: Audie Murphy, Dan Duryea, Dianne Foster, Elaine Stewart, Brandon de Wilde.

55. VERTIGO. Paramount, 1958. (c) *Alfred Hitchcock*. Sp: Alec Coppel and Samuel Taylor, b/o novel by Pierre Boileau and Thomas Narcejac. Cast: Kim Novak, Barbara Bel Geddes, Tom Helmore.

56. BELL, BOOK AND CANDLE. Columbia, 1958. (c) *Richard Quine*. Sp: Daniel Taradash, b/o play by John Van Druten. Cast: Kim Novak, Jack Lemmon, Ernie Kovacs, Hermione Gingold, Elsa Lanchester, Janice Rule.

57. ANATOMY OF A MURDER. Columbia, 1959. *Otto Preminger*. Sp: Wendell Mayes, b/o novel by Robert Traver. Cast: Lee Remick, Ben Gazzara, Arthur O'Connell, George C. Scott, Eve Arden, Kathryn Grant, Joseph N. Welch.

58. THE FBI STORY. Warner Bros., 1959. (c) *Mervyn LeRoy*. Sp: Richard L. Breen and John Twist, b/o book by Don Whitehead. Cast: Vera Miles, Murray Hamilton, Larry Pennell, Nick Adams, Diane Jergens.

59. THE MOUNTAIN ROAD. Columbia, 1960. *Daniel Mann*. Sp: Alfred Hayes, b/o novel by Theodore White. Cast: Lisa Lu, Glenn Corbett, Henry Morgan, Frank Silvera.

60. TWO RODE TOGETHER. Columbia, 1961 (c) *John Ford*. Frank Nugent, b/o novel by Will Cook. Cast: Richard Widmark, Shirley Jones, Linda Cristal, John McIntire, Mae Marsh.

61. THE MAN WHO SHOT LIBERTY VALANCE. Paramount, 1962. *John Ford*. Sp: James Warner Bellah and Willis Goldbeck, b/o story by Dorothy M. Johnson. Cast: John Wayne, Vera Miles, Lee Marvin, Edmond O'Brien, Andy Devine, Ken Murray.

62. MR. HOBBS TAKES A VACATION. 20th Century-Fox, 1962. (c) *Henry Koster*. Sp: Nunnally Johnson, b/o novel by Edward Streeter. Cast: Maureen O'Hara, Fabian, John Saxon, Lauri Peters, John McGiver, Marie Wilson, Reginald Gardiner.

63. HOW THE WEST WAS WON. MGM, 1963. (c) *John Ford, George Marshall, Henry Hathaway*. Sp: James R. Webb. Cast: Debbie Reynolds, Carroll Baker, Karl Malden, Agnes Moorehead, Gregory Peck, George Peppard, John Wayne, Henry Fonda, Richard Widmark, Karl Malden.

64. TAKE HER, SHE'S MINE. 20th Century-Fox, 1963. (c) *Henry Koster*. Sp: Nunnally Johnson, b/o play by Phoebe and Henry Ephron. Cast: Sandra Dee, Audrey Meadows, Robert Morley, John McGiver, Philippe Forquet.

65. CHEYENNE AUTUMN. Warner Bros., 1964. (c) *John Ford*. Sp: James R. Webb, suggested by book by Mari Sandoz. Cast: Richard Widmark, Carroll Baker, Karl Malden, Sal Mineo, Dolores Del Rio, Ricardo Montalban, Gilbert Roland, Edward G. Robinson.

66. DEAR BRIGITTE. 20th Century-Fox, 1965. (c) *Henry Koster*. Sp: Hal Kanter. Cast: Fabian, Glynis Johns, Cindy Carol, Billy Mumy, John Williams, Brigitte Bardot.

67. SHENANDOAH. Universal, 1965. (c) *Andrew V. McLaglen*. Sp: James Lee Barrett. Cast: Doug McClure, Glenn Corbett, Patrick Wayne, Rosemary Forsyth, Katharine Ross.

68. THE FLIGHT OF THE PHOENIX. 20th Century-Fox, 1966. (c) *Robert Aldrich*. Sp: Lukas Heller, b/o novel by Elleston Trevor. Cast: Richard Attenborough, Peter Finch, Hardy Kruger, Ernest Borgnine, Ian Bannen.

69. THE RARE BREED. Universal, 1966. (c) *Andrew V. McLaglen*. Sp: Ric Hardman. Cast: Maureen O'Hara, Brian Keith, Juliet Mills, Don Galloway, David Brian.

70. FIRECREEK. Warner Bros.-Seven Arts, 1968. (c) *Vincent McEveety*. Sp: Calvin Clements. Cast: Henry Fonda, Inger Stevens, Gary Lockwood, Dean Jagger, Ed Begley, J. Robert Porter.

71. BANDOLERO!. 20th Century-Fox, 1968. (c) *Andrew V. McLaglen*. Sp: James Lee Barrett, b/o story by Stanley L. Hough. Cast: Dean Martin, Raquel Welch, George Kennedy, Andrew Prine, Will Geer.

72. THE CHEYENNE SOCIAL CLUB. National General, 1970. (c) *Gene Kelly*. Sp: James Lee Barrett. Cast: Henry Fonda, Shirley Jones, Sue Ann Langdon, Dabbs Greer.

73. FOOLS' PARADE. Columbia, 1971. (c) *Andrew V. McLaglen*. Sp: James Lee Barrett, b/o novel by Davis Grubb. Cast: George Kennedy, Strother Martin, Kurt Russell, Anne Baxter, Kathy Cannon.

INDEX

157

159

ABOUT THE AUTHOR

Howard Thompson is a staff reporter-reviewer of The New York Times and has worked for the newspaper for twenty-five years. He is a former chairman of the New York Film Critics.

ABOUT THE EDITOR

Ted Sennett is the author of *Warner Brothers Presents*, a survey of the great Warner films of the Thirties and Forties, and of *Lunatics and Lovers*, on the years of the "screwball" movie comedy. He has also written about films for magazines and newspapers. He lives in New Jersey with his wife and three children.